Praise for *Memoirs of the Soul*...

"Highlighting the differences between autobiographical writing and memoir writing, Phifer urges amateur writers to write of the 'inner life,' or times of 'joy or crisis or profound contentment.' She offers a structured, well-organized process for writers to follow, which includes specific exercises, inspiring quotations, and examples of student work from her memoir-writing workshops…. This how-to is highly recommended for all public libraries."

—*Library Journal*

"The exercises in *Memoirs of the Soul* will challenge you to write with more depth, more sense of place, more feeling, and will give your writing an emotional impact that it lacked before."

—**Sue Bronson**, *Writers NW*

"Phifer's carefully phrased prompts, instructions, and examples ask writers to begin at the surface of their existence and to burrow deeper and deeper into their hearts and minds. With each chapter, she challenges would-be memoirists to take another step inward, to inch closer to their own souls. In many ways, Phifer's book is like a deep-sea diving expedition—or an archaeological dig—where the depth of the self is revealed layer by layer, league by league, chapter by chapter."

—**Professor W. Keith Duffy**
The Journal of the Assembly for Expanded Perspectives on Learning

"*Memoirs of the Soul* will be forever on my recommended lists for emerging memoirists who have trouble getting to the core of their stories and for more advanced writers who simply need to be inspired."

—**Carolyn Howard-Johnson**
Speaker, actor, author, and writing consultant

"*Memoirs of the Soul* approaches the writing of a spiritual autobiography in an organic, nonlinear way. Rather than simply listing the external events that mark a life in chronological fashion (I was born, I went to school, I got married, went to work,), *Memoirs* encourages the writer to follow threads of desire, passion, grief, awe, love, and sorrow that make up the spiritual life."

—*Presence: An International Journal of Spiritual Direction*

"Ordinary people now write their autobiographies as a matter of course, whether for publication or for their families, and Nan Phifer has written a splendid guide. Anyone wishing to delve into spiritual, creative, or transformational matters will do well to purchase her book."

—**Linda Hutton**
Hutton Publications

"'I have no inner life'—'Yes you do,' Phifer says, and she's got the idea-generating strategies and writing prompts to prove it."

—*The Oregonian*

"This useful jewel of a book will enhance both personal growth and writing skills."

—**R. John Allcorn**
National Review Network

"I was impressed with this book because it doesn't just tell how to write a memoir. It helps readers explore themselves in such a way that their writing gains more depth. It is full of exercises that can increase the vitality and impact of personal writing, and can help one's writing become more vivid and descriptive. Whether you are a new or experienced writer, this book will leave you itching to write!"

—**Novice Alicia Kleiman, OSB**
Shalom Prayer Center

"It is a how-to guide on writing that is also an escort for the great voyage of the soul. It reminds me of the examen process of Saint Ignatius of Loyola. Simple, profound, and a pathway to living a life of wholeness and balance."

—*Tune In!*

"Step-by-step strategies to help you begin, persist, and complete the process of moving to the center of your 'spiritual labyrinth'…. Although I usually find how-to books tedious at best, this one is so animated and evocative I am seriously thinking about embarking on the voyage."

—**G. Richard Wheatcroft**
The Center for Progressive Christianity

"*Memoirs of the Soul* encourages you to write about the times of wonder in your life: your strength, creativity, resilience, and moments of transformation. Doing so will allow you to breathe new life into personal memories, stimulate spiritual growth, and develop profound connections to the special places and people who have touched your heart."

—*Family Chronicle*

"Nan Phifer's book has one major problem—the title. Though technically correct, it leads bookstores and libraries to place her book in their spiritual or inspirational sections. Once you open the covers of this book, you'll realize it is a book for writers—all writers."

—*The Senior Times*

"Excellent guide if you have a personal story to tell. The author leads you through your life to discover aspects of experiences you have forgotten. Offers instruction, examples, writing exercises. Helpful also if you write other people's life stories."

—*Freelance Writer's Report*

"*Memoirs of the Soul* offers inspiration for self-reflection, whether one currently has the time to write or not. Phifer also offers suggestions on how this book can be used by one person, partners in writing, or in a group workshop setting."

—*Spiritual Woman Newsletter*

"In Phifer's book, the promise is that one will discover the most important goals of one's life, one's strengths and commitment to reach these goals, and a new sense of integration. According to Phifer, writing about one's spiritual life is a great adventure, one that facilitates open communication and an unsurpassed intimacy."

—*The Positive Aging Newsletter*

"*Memoirs of the Soul* by Nan Phifer is a must read for soul-searching through writing. As a librarian of twenty-five plus years, I perused, read, and reviewed hundreds of books on writing. Coming upon Nan's book, I was thrilled because it stood out."

—**Leonard B. Felkey**
Librarian and author

"Nan Phifer is a stealth bomber. She sneaks in, appears sweet and gentle and lovely, but then opens us up, through writing, to our own explosive promise."

—**Kae Evensen**
Lutheran pastor

"This book draws writers with soft encouragement and leads by respectful urging to the edge of remembrance. Then the prompts say, 'Jump!' and writers leap off a cliff into a vivid reliving of past experiences, which write themselves onto the page."

—**José McCarthy**
Psychiatrist

"[The] chapters, each with several writing prompts, encourage you to gradually go deeper into your psyche. The end result is a picture of not only the person you were but also the person you have become."

—**Judith Helburn**
Story Circle Network

"The book works like a guide, systematically and logically presenting the steps of organizing one's thoughts and setting them to paper."

—*The Flame*

"The lessons are often deep, and you may find out a lot more about yourself than what you set out to do."

—Kathleen Spring
Director, Writing Retreats for the Mind & Spirit

"Memoirs by definition tend to be rote and rife with nothing but facts and places. This publication… helps you put a perspective on your life you may not have known existed. This book also provides the tools to begin writing your own memoir from a more 'whole' place."

—Ann Downing
Sumi-e artist

"Nan Phifer, a gifted writer and teacher, provides a myriad of well-organized progressive steps and visual tools…. *Memoirs of the Soul* is a must for those wishing to see and appreciate their unique and divine contribution."

—Sarah Miller
Unity of the Valley Bookstore
Eugene, Oregon

MEMOIRS OF THE SOUL

MEMOIRS OF THE SOUL

A WRITING GUIDE

NAN MERRICK PHIFER

FOREWORD BY HAL ZINA BENNETT

IP INGOT PRESS

Eugene, Oregon

Published by: Ingot Press
P.O. Box 40025
Eugene, OR 97404
www.Ingotpress.com

Edited by Michelle Howry, Meg Leder, Ellen Kleiner, and Veronica Yates
Designed by Janice St. Marie
Cover art by Melinda Mendenhall
Production coordinated by Blessingway Authors' Services

Printed and bound in the United States of America

Library of Congress Cataloging-in-Publication Data
Phifer, Nan Merrick
Memoirs of the soul : a writing guide / by Nan Merrick Phifer.
cm.
Includes bibliographical references and index.
ISBN 978-0-9842060-0-1
Spiritual biography—Authorship. 2. Spiritual journals—Authorship. 3. Autobiography—Authorship. I. Title.

BL628.5.P55   2010   2009936188
808'.066158—dc21   CIP

10 9 8 7 6 5 4 3 2 1

FOR G. RICHARD WHEATCROFT

Wise mentor and gentle guide

ACKNOWLEDGMENTS

I'm indebted to the people who made the writing of this book possible.

The people who taught me: Nat Teich, recently retired director of the Oregon Writing Project at the University of Oregon, through whom I gained expertise in methods of teaching composition; Mary K. Healy, Associate Director of the University of California Bay Area Writing Project (BAWP), who conveyed the theory of the writing process with unusual clarity; and Keith Caldwell, also of the BAWP and provider of ingenious, infallible ideas for instruction;

The department heads at Lane Community College, who encouraged my professional growth: Dick Earl, Lance Reuther, and Pat John;

The many workshop participants, too numerous to name, who piloted the manuscript of this book and those who allowed me to publish excerpts from their writings;

The writers and teachers who critiqued my manuscript and made insightful suggestions: Jane Tompkins, Anne Beaufort, Susan Mosedale, Lisa Rosen, Robbie Pinter, Lowell A. Thomas, John Creger, Doug Finn, and Winthrop Griffith;

The scholars who examined this book to see if I had inadvertently been insensitive to beliefs and feelings of people whose faiths I don't know well: Tamman Adi, Imam and Director of an Islamic Cultural Center; Ernie Rimmerman, member of a Buddhist priory; and Shobhana Rishi, authority on Hinduism; as well as shamanic practitioner Alida Birch and musical healer Sharon Franklin;

The publishing experts: Elizabeth Lyon, authority in preparing book proposals; my editors at Writer's Digest Books, Michelle Howry and Meg Leder, who sensitively made subtle improvements; and Ellen Kleiner of Blessingway Authors' Services, an invaluable, dynamic catalyst in the republication of this book;

The editors: Lynwood Wilson, who streamlined a broadly inclusive chapter, and Veronica Yates, whose deft expertise kept on track both the vision and execution of the second edition.

Most of all I am grateful for the astute suggestions of my son, Matthew Rendall, and the support of my husband, Bob Phifer.

CONTENTS

PART III
CLIMAXES AND REVELATIONS

PART IV
THE REWARDS

FOREWORD

Where to begin!

How many times as a writer have I considered those three words? They come up whenever I sit down to write a new article or book. But nowhere are those words asked more often than when we sit down to write about our own lives. Where do we begin to write a memoir? One would think that anything autobiographical would be easy enough. After all, it's our own life story we're writing. We should know it backward and forward. Only when we sit down at the keyboard, or take up pen and paper to record it, do we discover how difficult it is. As author Walter Wellesley Smith once said, "There's nothing to writing. All you do is sit down . . . and open a vein."

Like all authors, I draw a great deal from the experiences of my own life. I travel back in my mind to an event that illustrates something I wish to say. And as often as not, the same old conundrum starts again—where to begin!

We think we have a clear mental picture, an emotional if not intellectual grasp of our past. Yet starting points elude us. When did my love of the sea begin? The first time I looked over the railing of a ship, probably clinging to the hem of my mother's dress? The first time I stood at the edge of Lake Michigan as a child, feeling the gentle waves lapping at my toes? Or with the first boat I owned, an old wooden rowboat that, adrift on the lake, I'd claimed as my own in the last days of summer when I was fourteen? Each experience of our lives seems to have many beginnings. And too often in our efforts to find them we become discouraged and back away from the writing that would otherwise bring us so much joy.

There have been numerous books about writing memoirs, a literary form that in recent years has gained great popularity. Many have extolled the benefits of this venture, of exploring the purpose and meaning, the joys, the sadness, the successes and disappointments of our lives. But Nan Merrick Phifer's *Memoirs of the Soul* is the first book I've found that lays out the practice of reaching into ourselves, finding the events that have been most meaningful, and having identified them, knowing where to begin committing ourselves to paper.

When I first picked up Nan's book and began flipping through the pages, my immediate reaction was, "I wish I'd had this book decades ago, when I first decided I wanted to be an author." Here are the essentials, all that's needed for the foundation upon which to build a memoir or autobiography. This is a nuts-and-bolts sort of book that, like a great tour guide, points a finger and says, "Look right there! Do you see that little wrinkle on the waves?" And there, moments later, the whale breaches and you are thrilled.

Nan has found the themes that take us to the inner ocean of our own consciousness, without making a big deal of it—and, perhaps more importantly, without losing the magic. Whether it's exploring the soul of a child (chapter 6), encountering the numinous (chapter 23), or revising your rough draft (chapter 28), there's wisdom, support, and secure guidance here that comes from one who knows of what she speaks. As comprehensive as Nan's instructions are, what's clear throughout is that each of us has our own unique story to tell; and while she may point and tell us exactly where to look, we always know that the only story we have to tell is our own and it is there that we find the greatest rewards.

Is there anything left out that I, as an author and writing coach, would add? I honestly don't think so. There aren't many books I can say this about. *Memoirs of the Soul* is a wonderful guide that tells us not only how to write the stories that only we can tell but how to journey within to the mysteries of our own special beginnings.

—**Hal Zina Bennett**
Author of *Write From the Heart* and *Write Starts*

PREFACE

Memoirs of the Soul goes beyond being a how-to book on memoir writing. It takes you on a journey into your own life that will reveal aspects of your experience you never knew existed. The author gives you all the nuts and bolts—writing prompts, warm-ups, creative exercises, doing first and second drafts, suggestions for revision, instruction on how to give and get feedback, and lots of emotional support—the practical things writers need in order to get started and make progress. But the true gift of the book is the way it introduces you to yourself.

Most people who set out to write a memoir have some kind of story to tell: memories of crucial events, interpretations of their own and other people's behavior, some scenes from childhood or adolescence, perhaps a life-changing moment of realization. But the stories about ourselves we carry around in our heads often turn out to be surface accounts, convenient shorthand versions of much deeper realities. The work of writing a memoir is really the work of learning who you are. It's archaeology—dusty, dirty, and sweaty, though never tedious. Mainly what it takes is courage, to allow your mind to transport you where it wants to go once you've started to dig. That's where a book like this comes in. It's written by a person who has taken the journey herself and who has accompanied many other people on the way. So with her you are in good hands.

Gently and respectfully, Nan Merrick Phifer takes on the role of guide, asking you questions no one has ever put to you before, leading you to places in your own psyche you have never visited, opening landscapes of your history that you have never glimpsed, making you aware of dimensions of your being you have not realized were there. You do the work yourself, but she is there to show you the way. If you follow her leads faithfully, she will take you very far. And even if you don't, you'll come away from this book with a different sense of yourself, of who you've been and who you might become.

—Jane Tompkins, Ph.D.
University of Illinois in Chicago

PART I

Beginnings

CHAPTER 1

Memoir as Voyage into the Soul

External facts about a life can be researched generations later,
but the inner life is irrevocably lost unless written during one's lifetime.

THIS BOOK WILL enable you to record the voyage, not of your ego, but of your soul. Public records sketch the statistics of your physical existence, while photographs, certificates, and documents show how you appear to others and what you accomplished. However, unless you reveal the feelings and thoughts you had when you were filled with love, grief, satisfaction, longing—the great sweep of feelings that shaped your soul—few people will ever truly know you. This book will help you identify the vital elements of your inner life and write about them. Furthermore, the material you are about to write will not only produce a lasting, written account, but in the very process of writing, you are likely to discover previously unrecognized dimensions of spirituality in your life.

The word *spiritual* comes from the Latin word *spiritus*, meaning "breath," "breath of god," "inspiration." *Spiritual* as used in this book refers to the essential and activating principle at the center of your being, your intangible essence. It encompasses but is not limited to experiences traditionally thought of as religious. It refers to your inner life, the part that lives at your vital core providing the animating force within you.

The further limits of our being plunge, it seems to me, into an altogether other dimension of existence from the sensible and merely "understandable" world. Name it the mystical region, or the supernatural region, whichever you choose. So far as our ideal impulses originate in this region (and most of them do originate in it, for we find them possessing us in a way for which we cannot articulately account), we belong to

it in a more intimate sense than that in which we belong to the visible world, for we
belong in the most intimate sense wherever our ideals belong.

—WILLIAM JAMES
American philosopher and psychologist

A GRAND VOYAGE

The very writing of your memoirs will stimulate spiritual growth, for in articulating your ideals and your responses to the great events and formative influences in your life you will reveal your values, motives, beliefs, and hopes. Just as you'll discover the things in your life that matter most and the ways you've worked to advance them, you may also show the price you paid when they were ignored. Your personal traits and patterns will emerge, and you'll observe characteristics from deep within yourself. Strengths and dimensions not previously appreciated will become apparent. Later, when you compile and organize your memoirs, you may feel that you are reintegrating elements of yourself.

You'll also gain perspective on relationships between the events and people in your life. One of the workshop participants who followed the method presented in this book suddenly exclaimed that for the first time she understood why she had married her husband; in ways she had never consciously recognized, he was like her beloved grand-father. Someone else came to realize that for years she had carried a burden of guilt for a death that was beyond her control. Such insights are not uncommon.

Life can only be understood backwards;
but it must be lived forwards.

—SØREN KIERKEGAARD
Danish philosopher and religious thinker

First and foremost, the exploration of your spiritual life through writing will be a great adventure. Your writing will help clarify the meaning and purpose of your life, as well as reveal its underlying spiritual dimensions. If you wish, you will also produce a lasting, edited, well-written book of which you can be proud, a book that opens your life to the people who are dearest to you and makes possible communication and understanding that might otherwise never exist.

EARLIER VOYAGERS

The first-known spiritual autobiography in Western literature is *Confessions* by Saint Augustine. Subsequent writers include such people as Boethius, Jean-Jacques Rousseau, Thomas Merton, C. S. Lewis, Elie Wiesel, Harvey Cox, James Baldwin, Karen Armstrong, Alfred Kazin, and Maxine Hong Kingston.

Memoirs, however, are different from autobiographies. Autobiographies present broad overviews, while memoirs focus on only the hours and minutes that are keen in our lives—the times when we are most alive, when experiences penetrate to the quick. In these moments we define ourselves; the ways we respond reveal our souls. At such times—moments of joy or crisis or profound contentment—our individuality emerges distinctly, and we sometimes have a sense of context beyond ourselves.

If you wish to extend your memoirs into an autobiography, you can supplement the critical core chapters in this book by adding narrative data about external events. Such additions will not be difficult. The memoirs you'll write at this time will give heart and soul to your autobiography and ensure that it is engaging.

Memoirs are also different from journals. They are more selective. Memoirists focus on the most significant experiences in their lives and then organize the chapters in a sequence that tells a story; journals tend to log or record daily growth, musings, and insights. Memoirs, because of their story structure, feel whole rather than fragmentary. Also, memoirs are usually more polished than journals and can become an art form, a type of literature. Memoirists often want to edit and revise their work and have it proofread. They may even select photographs and other documents to insert and then construct a book. These works can be suitable for publication and often make extraordinary gifts.

YOUR ITINERARY

You'll find your way to the recesses of your soul by first writing about the experiences, people, and places most important in your life. Each chapter of this guide provides a strategy to help you identify those elements and readily write about them. Writing "prompts"—starters for sentences that lead into your memories—will guide you to times when you were filled with significant emotions. After you've written rough drafts, you may choose to examine them in light of questions suggested for reflection on the topic. The reflections will help you perceive spiritual aspects such as compassion, transformation, uncanny insight, grace, times when you were imbued with strength, were in communion with something beyond yourself, or sensed the divine. You may find that your writing already implicitly reveals such dimensions, or you may decide to add insights based on the reflections suggested in this book.

As you proceed, you will not write chronologically. The memoirs you're about to compose won't focus on where you were born, what schools you attended, or where you've lived. Other documents do that. Here you'll write about your inner life, the heart of your being, your essence. Not until *after* you've collected a series of writings will you organize them—possibly chronologically, possibly some other way. Chapter 27 suggests ways to arrange your chapters and write satisfying conclusions.

Because your approach will be to write about the critical experiences in your life rather than to render a chronological account, your writing will never plod. Because you'll not begin with "I was born…" and then cite many not very interesting facts, your chapters will be compelling from the first pages. Readers will feel involved as they move from one important and dramatic aspect of your life to another. Most of us wish we could see into the hearts of those we love, and we certainly would like to look back into the souls of our ancestors. Through your writing you will share the most interesting aspects of yourself with your descendants and other readers of your memoirs.

Many thoughtful people would like to write about their most meaningful experiences but don't know where to begin or how to proceed. Because the undertaking seems over-whelming, they procrastinate and write little or nothing. However, by following the steps suggested in this guide, you will produce a collection of writings about your inner life.

WRITING TO THE CENTER

Each chapter provides step-by-step directions to assure that inexperienced writers as well as those with experience can produce writing of high quality. Chapters are ordered to progress from subjects easiest to write about and share with others to subjects that might be daunting if not preceded by the earlier chapters.

The early chapters begin with your outer life—the people, places, and events that shaped you. Although you'll select subjects from those accessible, factual realms, a series of questions will help you reflect on and write introspectively about the spiritual dimensions of those realms. Later chapters will enable you to write directly about your deepest emotions such as love, suffering, and ecstasy. If you've already written a reflec-tive family history, you may prefer to skip ahead to the advanced chapters. Write in the order that best serves your purpose.

The course your voyage will follow will not be linear. Autobiographies tend to be linear, starting with birth and moving year by year to the time the autobiography was written. Your memoirs, moving from your outer life toward your inner life, will spiral inward. If the word *voyage* evokes images of ocean travel, it is time to broaden your concept of the word, for voyages can be over land and into space as well. Visualize the map for your journey as a great labyrinth in space.

THE LABYRINTH MAP

Labyrinths, or mazes, are ancient patterns of paths along which one progresses from an opening at the outer edge into lanes that circle, turn back, resume direction, and make unexpected twists—all the while bringing the walker from the outer entrance toward the center. One of the earliest labyrinths was constructed in Egypt for the tomb of King Perabsen, circa 3400 BCE. A well-known mythological labyrinth was in the Cretan palace where Theseus killed the Minotaur. Indoor and outdoor labyrinths have been built all over the world. The drawing depicted in figure 1 shows a labyrinth paved with blue and white stones in the Cathedral of Chartres, completed in the thirteenth century in France.

Figure 1

Medieval labyrinths were thought of as paths leading us to our own spiritual centers. In a similar way, your writing will lead you from your outer life into your spiritual center. Moreover, as walkers in a physical labyrinth can turn back to retrace their steps and linger along the way, you too may return to earlier chapters to write about more of the many topics you will have generated. Unlike the walkers of labyrinths, you will not return the way you entered. When you've written into the heart of your memoirs, you will have arrived at your destination.

People who walk through physical labyrinths report surprise at the twists, turns, and resulting feelings of disorientation that frequently produce insights and discoveries. Upon reaching the center, many walkers experience a soothing sense of wholeness and balance. As your writing moves from your outer to your inner life, may you gain insights, make discoveries, and arrive at a sense of balance and wholeness.

"PROMPTS" PROVIDE AN EASY LAUNCH

"Prompts" will evoke your flow of words. Always feel free to rephrase the writing prompts to fit your individual life and way of speaking. When workshop participants first consider the prompts, they typically react blankly for a few minutes, then begin to write haltingly, and soon accelerate into a flow of writing. Strive to scrawl a rapid rough draft without pausing to consider what you're saying. Writing that springs uncensored from the subconscious onto the page is often revealing and insightful. One workshop participant said, "Nan, your prompts are like a can opener." Always allow the flow of your writing to take you wherever it goes; when it strays far from the prescribed subject, you may make stunning discoveries. The prompts are simply catalysts. No matter how you use them, you're "doing it right."

Moreover, if you use this book in the company of other writers you'll find their drafts to be more stimulating than any written prompt could be. Upon hearing what fellow writers have written, you'll often think, "Yes, of course!" and immediately know what in your own life must be told that would otherwise go unnoticed. To provide you with inspiration, ideas, and examples, this guide contains excerpts from the drafts of many people who, like you, are composing their memoirs.

A writer is not so much someone who has something to say as he is someone who has found a process that will bring about new things he would not have thought of had he not started to say them.

—WILLIAM STAFFORD
Poet Laureate of Oregon

This book provides the process.

CHAPTER 2

Modus Operandi

Ultimately, if the [writing] process is good,
the end will be good. You will get good writing.
—NATALIE GOLDBERG
American author

WE NOW KNOW that to write well we must be free to write badly. In the past, a common misconception stymied aspiring writers: they assumed that as they wrote they should choose the right words and spell and punctuate correctly. Those writers did not differentiate between a rough draft and a final draft.

Writers were liberated when it was shown that the best first drafts are filled with errors because we focused on what we were saying, not on how we were saying it. The first draft should capture ideas while they flit through our minds. We must not turn our attention from *what* we are writing to *how* we are writing because if we pause, our thoughts escape. While we puzzle over word choices and spellings, the rich feelings, perceptions, and ideas within us slip away. We must write quickly in order to include everything we have to tell.

The messy first draft, a rough draft, is later revised and proofread, but first the writer tries to be sure the ideas are complete and clear. The best way to do this is to hear the draft. We can read it to an attentive, nonjudgmental friend; we can ask someone to read it aloud to us; or we can simply read it aloud to ourselves. Any of these techniques affords perspective. Inevitably, we hear phrases that don't sound right, and we even "hear" what we inadvertently left out. Sometimes we hear that the impression made by the writing is not what we intended. Once we know what needs to be fixed, we can add to, change, rearrange, or delete what we wrote. As we do this, we're still working on content and should not be distracted by the mechanics of spelling, punctuation, or grammar. When we hear what we have written, we gain a new perspective; and upon seeing our content from an outside angle, we can reenvision it.

To write introspectively, memoirists need the freedom to make mistakes with content as well as with mechanics. After a draft is completed, it's not unusual for the writer to read it, reconsider, and conclude that the account gave the wrong impression or was somehow untrue to the experience. Memoirists, like philosophers and others who discover as they compose, need freedom to err and revise as they write.

Writers who work together in critiquing groups read their first drafts to one another, hear how they sound, and ask each other for suggestions. Writers working alone benefit from reading their rough drafts aloud to themselves, or to the cat, or by recording them and listening to the tape. Any oral reading and listening assists in the revising process.

After you have revised the content of your rough draft, you're ready to proofread it. If you are on a computer, use its spellchecker, but remember that spellcheckers only catch misspelled words; they do not distinguish between "here" and "hear," for example. If you're uncertain about your choice of words, punctuation, or paragraphing, you can ask someone to proofread for you. However, unless you plan to publish your memoirs, don't let concerns about mechanics be overriding, and certainly don't let them stop you from your undertaking. Your close friends and family will be glad to have your memoirs, whether or not they contain mechanical errors.

THE WRITING PROCESS
General Guidelines

The following steps of the writing process will be helpful as you write each chapter of your memoirs. Mark the next page with a Post-it so you can readily refer to it.

Starting with chapter 4 of this book, each chapter will begin with a preliminary warm-up writing, followed by a second writing. The warm-up writing will awaken your mind and stimulate your fluency. It will serve to propel your writing, and usually it will initiate subjects you'll want to develop further. If you are writing independently, you'll probably want to revise, proofread, and write the final version of your warm-up writing before going on to the second writing. However, if you are working along-side other writers you'll want to set the first rough draft aside for completion later and proceed with the others to the second writing. The first four steps of the writing process—gathering ideas, telling your story, writing your rough draft, and listening to it—are interactive. People writing in groups will want to do those steps while they are together, but you can complete the last three steps—revising, proofreading, and writing an improved final draft—apart from your group.

Some topics presented in this guide develop better for certain individuals than for others. Writers are often surprised when an unpromising prompt leads into a full, rich chapter, while another rough draft may remain meager. Because this book approaches each chapter subject in two different ways, at least one of your drafts will thrive and

Steps of the Writing Process

The following approach usually facilitates good writing. If it does not help you, feel free to make alterations. This approach is meant as a general guide, not a constraining formula.

1. **Gather ideas.** Using memory aids such as photographs, documents, souvenirs, maps, lists, and graphs, as well as other idea-gathering strategies, you'll find that your life abounds with subjects. Record your ideas, select one to cultivate, and store the remaining ideas in a "greenhouse" file.

2. **Tell a friend** or writing partner the story you are considering writing. Narrating it orally before writing it will help you organize your ideas and find words to express them.

3. **Scrawl a quick rough draft,** skipping lines so you will have room to revise. Putting fluency first, ignore spelling and punctuation; you'll proofread for mechanics later. Number pages. Dare to ramble. Pursue your thoughts without concern for mechanical correctness.

4. **Listen to the rough draft.** Read it aloud to yourself, a dear friend, or a response group. Any listening can help you find out if you conveyed what you intended to.

5. **Revise the rough draft** if you wish, clarifying, restating, adding, or deleting information. Your revision may or may not be influenced by listeners' responses.

6. **Ask someone to proofread** for you if you are concerned about punctuation, grammar, or spelling. If you write your final drafts on a computer, take advantage of the spellchecker.

7. **Handwrite, type, or key in a final draft.**

flourish, and usually both will. The second writing is designed to develop more fully than the first, but the warm-up writing sometimes supersedes it.

Your Greenhouse File

Keep a manila folder or a section of your notebook as a "greenhouse" file. This "holding bed" is a place to store ideas for later chapters and to "plant" drafts you don't like, stunted beginnings, and even unexpected inspirations. Sometimes an idea forms when we don't have time to put it in writing. Store the idea, the seed, in your greenhouse file along with the various beginnings that need germination time. Later you can remove anything that looks promising and give it a new opportunity to flourish in whatever form it takes.

The Rough Draft

A successful technique for writing rough drafts is to skip lines so you'll have space to rewrite sentences and insert new ones. Packages of ordinary, lined notebook paper are ideal, but some writers prefer cheap spiral notebooks or legal pads. Choose any sort of paper on which you can skip lines, make insertions, and write error-strewn impulsive drafts. Before beginning to write, make an X in the left margin of every other line as a reminder to write on alternating lines. You may feel you're using lots of paper, but you'll need room to write in changes and additions.

Write on only one side of the paper so you can later cut pages apart to insert and rearrange paragraphs. You cannot cut and paste if you write on the back.

Number pages, and even identify them with a chapter number or subject word so you can reassemble them more easily if they become shuffled. Of course, if you are using a computer many of these arrangements will automatically be taken care of.

We all have our individual habits and quirks and may not feel fluent unless we approach our writing in a familiar way. Therefore, consider the advice in this book and then do what will work best for you.

The Final Draft: A Lasting Book

Not every voyager cares about creating a book. The expedition, the discoveries that come from the writing itself, is the great adventure. You are no less a traveler if you do not produce a book for others to read; however, many voyagers do find satisfaction in polishing their first drafts and leaving a lasting account. Just as you would value a book written by one of your ancestors centuries ago, the memoirs you are writing now may someday be of keen interest to your great-great-great-grandchild. You may even decide to publish copies for a broader community.

Ordinary paper becomes brittle and crumbly after about thirty years, but acid-free paper will last for three hundred years. You can find it at stationery or art supply stores. The store where you purchase paper may sell several qualities that range in price; the least expensive will serve well as long as it is labeled "acid free." Handwrite, type, or key in your final version onto the acid-free paper. When making copies of your memoirs, you may need to bring your own acid-free paper to the copy shop.

Leave space to insert photographs, clippings, and documents you want to include. Those pictures and other items will be preserved when copied onto the acid-free paper. If you like to sketch, consider embellishing your book with drawings and ornamentation.

Office supply stores carry a variety of binders, some inexpensive and some costly. Choose according to your preference and means, and consider making copies of your memoirs for the people to whom you feel close. It is the most personal gift you can give and will be increasingly treasured by the people who come to know you through your book, perhaps long after your lifetime.

OBSTACLES YOU MAY ENCOUNTER
Procrastination

"Tomorrow. Tomorrow I'll really sit down and write. Next week. Next year. After I do the dishes, mow the lawn, fix the faucet, watch a TV show."

To be able to write your spiritual memoirs, however, you must first be convinced of the worth of your undertaking. If you feel dubious about it, then you'll give priority to routine chores and passive pleasures. Sitting down to write won't just happen; you have to resolve to make it happen.

Many writers benefit from keeping a schedule. They reserve certain hours of every day or every week for writing. To succeed with a schedule, to be able to decline tempting invitations and distractions without hesitation, you must first believe in the merits of your project. Then earnestly ask your family and friends not to interrupt you during your time for writing.

Another way many writers conquer procrastination is by scheduling regular meetings with a small group of other writers. At these meetings everyone reads from a work in progress. Knowing that fellow members expect everyone to bring a draft to read provides strong incentive to produce writing. For suggestions about how to write with companions or colleagues, see chapter 30.

A rigid writing schedule and regular meetings are arbitrary structures, but they do help many successful writers accomplish their goals. If we wait for the muse to whisper in our ears, we may never do more than intend to get around to writing tomorrow or next week or next year.

Honor the grand voyage of writing your spiritual memoirs. Most people have never considered doing what you are about to do. It isn't frivolous, easy, or trivial. Close the door to the room in which you write, unplug the telephone, breathe deeply and slowly, and in a prayerful manner approach each day's writing. Award-winning science fiction writer Bruce Holland Roger has taped a motto to his computer that says, "I am an angel in disguise writing a holy text." He chuckles as he tells this, yet he believes in the significance of his work. You are undertaking the writing of your spiritual memoirs, a profoundly meaningful project, so find symbols for your workspace, create rituals for yourself, respect your writing schedule, and your success will not be waylaid by procrastination.

Negative Criticism

Criticism from contemporaries is of greater concern to memoirists and autobiographers than to most other writers. We worry about what our families will think and how listeners and readers will evaluate not only the writing but our lives and ourselves as individuals. These worries can become debilitating. If we dwell on them, our writing will be stunted.

For memoirs to be genuine and deep, your writing must be as candid as possible. Write your first draft for yourself alone. Write honestly. If your writing is intended only for yourself and, perhaps, a few selected friends, then you are free of concern. However, if you are writing for members of your family, for your community, or for broad publication at a later time, before you write your final draft you can decide whether to edit out parts that might cause harm or distress.

Frequently, the information we feel guilty about revealing actually ends up eliciting sympathy from readers. For the first time, readers understand our intentions, our problems, and our regrets. They usually respond with compassion.

At all stages of your writing you'll have the option of sharing or not sharing your writings with friends and fellow writers. If you are writing with a partner or workshop participants, you may always say, "This time I'll pass" when it is your turn to read. Step four of the writing process suggests that you read your rough draft to listeners. To encourage your listeners to respond constructively, give them the guidelines on page 33. At the top of the guidelines is the Chinese symbol for "listen." The left section denotes an ear, while parts of the right section indicate "you," "undivided attention," and "heart." Be guided by this wisdom. Listen earnestly from your heart.

Groups of writers who follow the guidelines for listeners ensure that the response group is safe, supportive, and constructive. This procedure has been repeatedly tested and found reliable. In groups that have not followed these guidelines, uncomfortable feelings have occasionally festered. So please mark the guidelines for easy reference or make copies to avoid potential difficulties.

A few words of encouragement for those who may be writing independently: If you are writing alone, without the support of a writing group or colleagues, you can still take advantage of the guidelines for listeners by responding in the recommended way to your own drafts. Acknowledge the strength of your drafts, and then stop to wonder what questions a listener who doesn't know you might have. Often, we inadvertently omit essential information when we fail to ponder what a stranger might want to know about us.

Guidelines for Listeners

- **Listen** with a nonjudgmental, open mind.

- **Listen** to learn.

- **Remain** totally, unfailingly confidential about what you hear.

To respond constructively:

- **Describe what you like** about the writing. Point out a strength in either the content or manner of writing. Always do this first.

- **Second, ask a question** about something the writer did not tell.

Now you, the listener, have said enough. Unless the writer asks your opinion about something else, say no more.

Concern about Mechanical Correctness

Writers should never hesitate to write their memoirs because they cannot spell or do not understand grammar and punctuation. Poignant, priceless memoirs have been written by unschooled writers. The thoughts and feelings of the writer are what matter most. The people who love you will overlook or will notice your mechanical errors; either way, they will be grateful to you for proceeding to write your memoirs.

Look at the proofreading tips in chapter 29 for ways to proof your rough drafts before writing your final versions.

Questions about Regionalisms

Memoirists sometimes wonder if they should drop their regionalisms. The answer is no! The locale where you grew up has flavored who you are. If, when you write, you "reckon" or "hanker," and you call the frying pan a "spider" or use "gum bands" rather than rubber bands, include these terms. To whitewash them out of your memoirs would be to erase a part of yourself. If you were writing a technical report or an academic essay, then you would replace your regionalisms, but if you were doing that kind of writing you wouldn't be writing about yourself.

The daughter of one writer I worked with said she intended to read only the first chapter of her father's memoirs before going to bed. When she began reading, however, she "could hear Dad talking" and was unable put his book down until she had read all of it.

FINAL PREPARATIONS

Notice the suggested readings at the end of the book. This list is a resource for people who write alone or with informal groups, as well as for people who teach or enroll in memoir-writing classes. As you scan the authors' names, be aware that by writing your spiritual memoirs, you are joining an esteemed company.

Use *Memoirs of the Soul* as a manual, a travelers' guide that you will follow step-by-step to the center of your spiritual labyrinth. Along the way you'll find two kinds of guideposts: one identifies where you are along the steps of the writing process and the other leads you through the labyrinth. If you sometimes feel jerked about, have faith that these twists and turns will eventually bring you to a place you could not have reached by a direct path; each lane you explore will prepare you for the next.

READY TO EMBARK

You are about to launch forth on a grand adventure, a voyage of discovery through writing. As you reflect on the most important dimensions of your life, you'll gain new perspectives and insights. Moreover, because questing writers don't know exactly what they'll find until they write, you're likely to surprise yourself. You'll write both to discover and to record your very essence—the inner workings of your soul.

Whether you write independently, with a partner, or as part of a writing group depends on your personal preference and circumstances. Some people prefer the privacy and tranquility of writing individually, while others find interaction with fellow writers to be stimulating and helpful. If you decide to write with colleagues or a friend, please see chapter 30 at this time.

You are now ready to make a spiritual voyage and, if you wish, to produce memoirs that will enable the people you love to see into your heart and mind.

Please step aboard!

CHAPTER 3

Subjects for Your Memoirs

The heart has its reasons, which reason does not know.

—Blaise Pascal
French religious thinker, mathematician, physicist

MAY I USE the pronoun I?

Am I important enough to write about my own life?

Do I have enough to say?

Yes to all these questions.

One of the first questions some beginning memoirists ask is "May I use the pronoun *I*?" People who ask this question probably were instructed by their teachers to avoid using the first person, but the kinds of assignments being taught to them were most likely reports and impersonal essays. Memoirs are a different genre. The pronoun *I* is correct for all personal writing.

Deeply moving, meaningful memoirs have been written by people who are not famous or important in a public way. The writing of spiritual memoirs has nothing to do with celebrity status or worldly achievements. Memoirs are about our ideals and intentions, the longings and laughter that have filled our hearts, the love we have felt, the compassion we have received and given, the moments when we have been graced, and when we have transcended ourselves. These experiences have little or nothing to do with status. As you write reflectively on your inner life, you will discover your spiritual importance.

You have much to say. An idea-gathering exercise in each chapter of this guide will bring forth such an array of significant personal subjects that you'll be surprised at how many important memories you have to write about. Each topic could develop into a chapter or a section of a chapter. This chapter will prove to you that your life is so filled with subjects, you'll have to be selective.

The first step of the writing process is to capture ideas. Idea-gathering strategies in each chapter will draw key words from your life, words that identify the text of your life.

One way to discover subjects for your memoirs is to name the people, places, activities, things, and experiences you "hold in your heart."

On an $8\frac{1}{2} \times 11$-inch (22×28 cm) sheet of paper, draw a valentine-shaped heart large enough to fill the page. Don't be concerned if it's lopsided or askew; real hearts aren't valentine-shaped anyway. If you are anatomically minded, draw your heart more egg shaped, the shape of a real human heart.

Next, you'll respond to the suggested prompts and soon begin to fill your heart with words. If your heart starts to overflow with words, write on the back of your page or draw a second heart on another page.

Inside the heart, name the following, as in figure 2, on page 38:

People who have been important to you
• They may be alive or dead, young or old.
• Their impact on you may have been good or bad.
• You may have been any age when they were important.
• Remember parents, friends, lovers, enemies, colleagues, employers, children, and others about whom you've felt emotion.

The idea-gathering strategies throughout this book are only that, strategies. If they prompt thoughts that go beyond the suggestions given, they are working well. The strategies are like flint whose purpose is to ignite your own memory and thought. Freely change or deviate from any suggestion in this book at any time.

When Geri Meyers filled in her heart during a workshop, she asked if a dog could be entered under "people." The answer is yes! Every idea for writing that arises from your life can be included. Later in this chapter you'll read what Geri wrote.

Places where significant events in your life occurred
• Geographic locations
    ~ Homes
    ~ Parks
    ~ Sanctuaries
    ~ Your personal retreat
    ~ A meeting place
    ~ A place where a dramatic event occurred
    ~ A place where you were very happy or miserable
    ~ If you think of big formations like cities, mountain ranges, and seashores, name the particular spot where you were.

- Institutions
    - ~ Schools
    - ~ Camps
    - ~ Places of worship
    - ~ Work sites
    - ~ Hospitals
- Interior spaces
    - ~ A bedroom
    - ~ A kitchen
    - ~ A childhood place where you played or hid
    - ~ A place like the backseat of an old Ford

Things you have valued or would be sorry to lose
- Belongings that have sentimental value
    - ~ Gifts
    - ~ Something made by hand
    - ~ An item associated with an important occasion
    - ~ Letters
    - ~ A trinket that reminds you of a good time
- Possessions that represent achievements
    - ~ Awards and trophies
    - ~ Things you worked for or saved money to buy
- Items that provide pleasure
    - ~ Musical instruments
    - ~ Sports equipment
    - ~ Particular books
    - ~ Shop or gardening tools, or a birdhouse

Activities or experiences that have been important to you
- Physical
    - ~ Hiking
    - ~ Camping
    - ~ Running
    - ~ Walking the dog
    - ~ Stacking wood
    - ~ Playing ball games
    - ~ Cycling
    - ~ Swimming
    - ~ Exercising

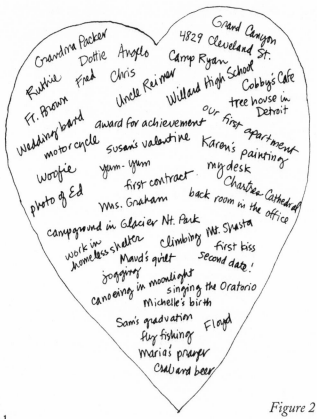

Figure 2

- Intellectual
    - ~ Reading
    - ~ Conversing
    - ~ Writing
    - ~ Taking classes
    - ~ Teaching
    - ~ Studying
    - ~ Thinking
    - ~ Discovering
- Emotional times
    - ~ Bliss or wretchedness
    - ~ Consuming fear, dread, or anxiety
    - ~ Tender love, peace, compassion, hope, longing
- Religious feelings
    - ~ Rituals you observe
    - ~ Meditation and personal prayers
    - ~ Experiences associated with beliefs and doubts
    - ~ Times of compassion and of grace
    - ~ Moments of transcendence

After you've filled in your heart with subjects, circle those you would like to include in your memoirs, either as topics for chapters or for parts of chapters. In choosing subjects, trust your intuition. Some subjects will pulse with more importance than others. A topic your family or acquaintances might consider important may not be as meaningful to you as other subjects. Be guided by your feelings.

From among the circled subjects, choose one you feel most inclined to write about today. It need not be the most significant subject or the most spiritual. In the coming weeks and months you'll have time to write about as many of these subjects as you wish. The best way to select the one to write about at this moment is to follow your enthusiasm since that's where your energy hovers.

John Pierce remembered a particular blind date as an emotional event. He married Lura four years later, and they are still lovingly married. Here is an excerpt from John's memoirs.

I first met her on a blind date. I had many blind dates. They were my norm. I joined a fraternity my freshman year in college, and all pledges were required to have at least two dates per week. Where I went to school I knew no one, for I had moved to Oklahoma the day following my graduation from high school. Being rather shy in the boy-meets-girl category, I considered blind dates my only alternative.

I breathed a sigh of relief when Christmas break came. It meant a two-week reprieve from that terrible awkwardness. However, one of my fraternity brothers came home with me to Bartlesville. The girl he was dating lived there, and my house became a convenient stopover for his romance.

Gene felt sorry for me. So did the young woman he was dating, and she had a friend. "You'll like her, she has a great personality," Tolly told me on the phone. (I'd been through this before.) "There is a Christmas dance, and we can arrange a date for you. Besides, Lura needs a date too."

"What's her name?"

"Lura."

"You mean Lora?…Laura?"

"No, Lura. It's a family name, I think."

"How tall is she?"

"Five nine."

"Too tall!"

"Come on, John. You'll like her. She's really funny."

I sighed. "Oh well, I guess it's something to do." Hanging up, I mumbled to myself, "I really don't want to do this again."

On that fateful night, Gene picked up Tolly first, and the three of us drove to Keeler Street to pick up my tall blind date with the different name. The driveway at 1940 Keeler led to a big, white, two-story house on a corner lot. On the left of the drive stood a glass greenhouse filled with all kinds of flowering plants that her mother and father grew as a hobby, and to make it a paying proposition some were sold to the community. The walkway from the drive led to the back door over which a porch light brightly burned. I felt apprehensive coming to the back door to ring the bell.

With fear and trembling I approached, and as I reached out to push the button for the bell I thought, "Why am I doing this? Life doesn't have to be this hard." I rang it anyway and stood there for what seemed like the longest and also the shortest wait of my life.

There she was, all five feet nine inches of her. Beautiful! ("Why does she need a blind date?") Large brown eyes; red, full lips; and a most marvelous smile!

"Yes," I thought. "Yes, indeed."

Velma Tweedie also met her spouse, Bill, on a blind date—one she had set up for a friend, but Velma and Bill were "taken with each other." They whispered throughout the movie the two couples had gone to see. After a year of courtship, Velma quit her job in a doctor's office to marry Bill. This is her recollection of their wedding day.

When the strains of "At Dawning" began, I emerged from the kitchen, my beautiful bridal bouquet of pink roses and stephanotis (made by my mother) shaking. My knees were, too.

The ceremony began. The minister's voice was booming, and I tried to concentrate on what he was saying. All was quiet until my small stepsister Bonnie wailed, "I don't want Velma to leave." Then I started to cry and, one by one, all the guests began to weep, even my former boss, our reserved and contained family doctor. All were weeping— that is, except the groom, who patiently waited for the tears to subside.

Our vows were finally sealed with the usual but damp kiss. The minister said it was the wettest wedding he'd ever witnessed.

After a beautifully planned and prepared luncheon given us by family and friends, we set off in our blue Chevrolet, with a rumble seat. We climbed the hill to the top of the picturesque rim rocks—the sun was shining, the snow melting—and we headed for Southern California on our honeymoon.

Suddenly the engine began to make queer, explosive noises, and smoke poured forth. On examination we found quantities of rice on the engine. Bill swept it out and we were on our way.

Once you have chosen from among the many subjects you named in your heart, you too, like Velma and John, will write about a vivid memory, though your story, whatever it is, will be different from theirs. You may write about a place you remember well, a person who made a difference in your life, or an experience you'll never forget. Your subject may be pleasant to remember or it could bring tears to your eyes. Choose from among the many subjects you named in your heart.

The most natural way to begin the flow of words is by telling your story before writing it. Speaking is more spontaneous than writing, so if you tell, even briefly, what you plan to write, you'll write with ease. If a suitable listener is not present, imagine telling your story to someone you love or to an interested, understanding individual.

For the moment, lay your pen aside. Visualize your friend waiting, listening, ready to hear what you will say. Notice how you would begin your story, what words you would use. Now pick up your pen and write those opening sentences on paper, knowing you can change them later. Even sentences that aren't very good can do the job well because they get you started.

Telling your story to a listener before beginning to write, or even imagining that you are telling it to a friend, will give your composition a sincere, personal tone. In the process, it will help you make a natural transition from speaking to writing.

Instructions for people writing with others appear in boxes throughout the remainder of this book. If you are writing independently, skip these boxed directions.

> If you're writing with a partner or group of writers:
>
> - Tell the story you plan to write.
> - Listen while the other person tells you the story she or he plans to write.

Keep in mind chapter 2 suggestions for writing successful first drafts. Only by writing several rough drafts on different subjects will you acquire the habit of skipping lines and using only one side of the paper.

Your first draft will flow more freely if you focus on content and ignore mechanics such as spelling, punctuation, grammar, and word choice. If you stop to wonder about those things as you are composing your ideas, your thoughts will be interrupted. Later when you proofread you'll attend to the mechanics of writing. Right now it's all right to have a draft filled with mechanical errors.

One good way to begin is with the words "When I was…" Let your readers know approximately how old you were and something about your circumstances. Orient them so they'll know how and where to visualize you, and then tell the story. Quickly write whatever comes to mind. Later you can insert additional information and make changes and corrections.

The length of your piece is determined by how much you have to tell. You might produce an entire chapter, or you might create a series of short sections on different topics. If you're writing alongside fellow writers, plan to write for twenty to thirty minutes, or until most people have paused.

Look back at what you have written, particularly to see if you told about your feelings. Sometimes writers tell what happened but forget to mention how they were affected by it. If necessary, when revising your rough draft insert information about your feelings.

Geri Meyers did tell how she felt when she was eight years old. She escaped a heavy atmosphere at home by riding her emerald green bicycle and taking her little dog, Moe, as a passenger in the wire handlebar basket.

Geri is currently researching her family's genealogy and writing her memoirs for her grandchildren.

I mounted my emerald charger, a means that carried my friend and me on an emotional cleansing. The wind washed us with an independence and carefree spirit my parents had long forgotten. I searched for the freedom to experience happiness free from my parents' anger, arguing, mistrust, and bitterness. I didn't know why they were that way. It was all I ever knew, but I yearned to be surrounded by joy, not heaviness. I remember at eight years old modestly expressing my one wish to my mother: "I wish I could be happy for one whole day." My parents' distance from each other permeated our home. But on my bike I was in control of its movement and my direction, which lightened my burdens.

Moe was a fifteen-pound toy terrier/Pomeranian mix. His short hair was fawn-colored with a white patch shaped like a diamond that marked his chest, and his naturally coiled tail was tipped with white as if dipped in paint. He looked like a soldier at attention. He was sitting with his chest bowed out, his head erect, and his ears straight up with attentiveness to my every word and so willing to please me. When I spoke, I had his undivided attention, and it gave me a feeling of worth.

I asked him, "Would you like to take a ride?" As he stood on all fours, his tail started to wag with an upbeat tempo, and his tongue popped out of his mouth as he panted in anticipation of the promised outing. He lifted his feet with excitement as though the cool grass were a bed of hot coals. It was a grand response of splendor when others I loved didn't have time for me. My handlebars supported a large woven wire basket. Moe was able to balance his small feet on the wires, but I learned to make the ride more comfortable for him by nesting the basket with my doll's blanket.

As we rode down the street with the breeze flowing over us, I had my head tilted back, my chin pointing out, while my nostrils enjoyed the freshness of a new day. I laughed because Moe had his head back, eyes shut, and his ears were flapping in the wind. We both thrived on those freeing moments and bonded with each venture.

After you've composed your rough draft, the next step is to listen to it. When you hear your rough draft, you'll gain a sense of how it affects others, whether it comes across the way you intended, and whether it's clear and complete. Professional writers usually work in critiquing groups, groups of writers who listen to each other's rough drafts and respond with their reactions and suggestions. Often they take turns meeting in their homes where they gather around the dining table or group themselves in the living room to hear and discuss their drafts. Compatible, constructive groups continue to work together for years.

If when you read your draft your listeners become confused or have questions, you'll realize what you need to do to make your story clear. If they don't share the emotion you meant to convey, you can determine where additional information is needed.

If you're writing independently, find a quiet, peaceful place where you can read aloud to yourself undisturbed, or find a dear friend who's willing to listen while you read your rough draft. Some writers tape-record their drafts so they can hear them. Reading your draft aloud, even without the benefit of listeners who respond, reveals ways you can improve it. You'll hear how you can make it better.

If you're writing with a large group, divide into subgroups of three or four and read to each other.

Most of us feel uneasy about reading our writing aloud. We feel vulnerable knowing we could be criticized. When we gave oral reports in school, our hearts probably banged and our stomachs cramped, even though those reports were about impersonal, factual information. Now you are being asked to reveal personal information about significant events in your life to people you might not know well. So that your audience understands the spirit in which they are to listen, tell them about the guidelines for listeners on page 33. Your listeners must agree to be nonjudgmental and supportive, to listen, to learn, and to guard the confidentiality of each reader.

Respond to each rough draft you hear by:

- First, telling what you like about it. What are its strengths? What did you admire?
- Then asking for further information. Writers often assume they've explained things they have left out. Your questions will help the writer know how to reinforce the draft.

Unless the writer asks for more suggestions, you've said enough. If the writer asks a specific question, try to answer it.

Your role is *not* to evaluate the actions or feelings of the writer.

When you read your rough draft aloud to yourself, and especially if you read it to someone else, you "viewed" it from another perspective. You reenvisioned it. The aural experience gives you insight into how to revise it. Think of the actual experience as the first experience. The experience you imagined when you heard your written description is the second, and somewhat different, experience. When we hear and imagine what we wrote, we perceive discrepancies between the two experiences and "see" what we need to do to mesh them, to bring them into alignment, to make the second experience true to the first. You may wish to add information, take something out, change words or phrases, or reorganize the sequence of your telling. Make any changes that will cause your story to be more understandable and accurate. Revise it.

Memoir writers often wonder if they may tell all they really experienced, thought, and felt, or if they should censor themselves. If you want to learn all you can about yourself, to really explore the depth of your soul, then write candidly and honestly. But if you are concerned about condemnation by readers or fear that what you say could harm someone else, then you must determine what to omit or, perhaps, alter. One practical approach is to write the rough draft as candidly as possible, let some time pass, and later decide whether to edit out any parts that concern you.

When you are satisfied that your rough draft does create the story you want to tell in the minds of listeners or readers, then you're ready to have it proofread. Our friends and families usually prefer that we write the way we speak, so concern about grammar may not be necessary.

However, if you would like help with the mechanics of standard English, ask a friend to check your:

- Paragraphing
- Punctuation
- Selection of words
- Capitalization
- Spelling

If you feel uneasy about your basic, overall proofreading skills, turn to the tips in chapter 29.

Now is the time to think of a title for the piece or chapter you have written. It can be as simple and straightforward as one word, or it can be fanciful. Think of Eudora Welty's title "Why I Live at the P.O.," Honoré de Balzac's "A Passion in the Desert," Dorothy Parker's "Big Blonde," and Seymour Freedgood's "Grandma and the Hindu Monk." Other intriguing titles imply answers: "The Reason I'm a Vegetarian," "Because My Watch Had Stopped," "Why I Dropped Out of High School." Ask the people who listened to your rough draft to suggest titles. Listeners are likely to name what they perceived as the theme of your writing, suggestions that frequently provide surprising insights for the writer. The reason titles are often created last is that we don't know exactly what we'll say or what its impact will be until after we've completed the writing.

At this time you're ready to write your final draft. Remember to use acid-free paper, and if you're writing by hand, you no longer need to skip lines.

Collect final drafts of all your chapters in a box or notebook where they'll be safe. Eventually you'll organize them, make a title page, write a conclusion, and bind your pages. Chapter 27 tells you how to assemble your own book.

The heart you filled with names of people, places, events, and important things can serve as a table of contents. Save it. Keep it in the loose-leaf notebook or manila folder you think of as your greenhouse file. In addition to storing ideas for further chapters, this file will also be a good place to "plant" unfinished rough drafts.

You've accomplished the hardest part—getting started—which is a barrier for many people. You've made the breakthrough! You found that you have numerous possible topics, and you've gone through the process of drafting, revising, and writing a final version. If you want to write about more of the subjects you circled in your heart, do so now, following the same process.

And now it [your heart] says: take it to the limit—
full-blown, like a spinnaker in front of you—
And it will be taken, and tested,
Touched, transfigured, stretched and tormented

Until you know its meaning is real,
is All.

—I CHING

Chinese Book of Changes, translated by Palmer, Ramsay, and Xiaomin

CHAPTER 4

Breathing Life into Your Writing

*A writer's problem does not change. He himself
changes and the world he lives in changes but his problem
remains the same. It is always how to write truly and, having
found what is true, to project it in such a way that it becomes
a part of the experience of the person who reads it.*

—Ernest Hemingway
American novelist and short story writer

CERTAIN EXPERIENCES REMAIN within us from the day they occurred throughout the rest of our lives. They formed us. They might be as small as the overhearing of a whispered sentence, but we recorded them in our memories, and they became part of who we are. In writing about these experiences, we understand them from a new perspective and may gain insights. By sharing these aspects of our inner lives with trusted friends, we allow them to truly know us.

This chapter demonstrates a technique for describing incidents so vividly that your readers will feel what you felt. You will write about a memorable experience in a way that will engage your readers. After that, you can employ the technique whenever you wish as you write your remaining memoir chapters.

Begin with a warm-up writing. As you write this rough draft, tell whatever comes to mind and write without concern for correctness. Write for about twenty minutes, using one of the following prompts:

- A day I'll never forget…
- An experience that made a great impact on me was…
- My pulse quickened when…

Read this rough draft aloud. The account you've just written may be one you'll enjoy sharing with a companion; if it is not, then read it aloud to yourself in a quiet, private place.

If you are writing with fellow writers, form small groups and listen to each other's drafts. Remember to listen respectfully, learn all you can, and never repeat what you hear.

Response suggestion:

- Point out a word, phrase, or sentence that remains most vivid in your mind.
- Then ask a question.

Wes Flinn gathered ideas for this description of a bagpiper by first systematically analyzing his sensory memories. A writer and teacher in Eugene, Oregon, he enjoys catching images with a camera, as well as with his pen.

> *My bride was walking toward me. I was unsure and shaky; thankfully, the bagpipes tethered me to the ground with tones of celebration. I was drawn back to the day we chose our piper.*
>
> *We found him at the end of a maze of rural Massachusetts roads: a staunch conservative with a raggedy, unruly beard and bits of lunch still clinging to the crevices between his teeth. He was a man fighting passionately for gun rights and freedom to do what the hell he likes at home. A self-proclaimed Rush Limbaugh listener and grower of his own food and hops for brewing, he also created his own kilts and piping garb. He walked around his yard, pipes blaring, letting their sounds of marching and the history of battlegrounds fill us with excitement and anticipation. Amy looked down and plucked a four-leaf clover from the overgrown grass by the woodpile. How can you turn your nose at such a clear sign? We hired John on the spot and were never sorry.*

Notice how effectively Wes included small details—the bits of food between the teeth and the four-leaf clover underfoot.

To prepare for your second rough draft, think of an experience you would like to relive, or one you wish had not happened, or one that made a difference in the way you think or feel about yourself. The subject you choose can be either positive or negative. The episode may have been traumatic or exhilarating, or it could be memorable for quiet, personal reasons. Any experience you've replayed in your mind has become part of you and can be an excellent subject choice.

A way to identify significant experiences is to list them:

Times when
- Your heart pounded
- Your stomach tightened
- Your skin tingled
- You held your breath
- You wept with joy, relief, grief, or sympathy

Experiences you would like
- To relive
- To erase

> *The best time for planning a book*
> *is while you're doing the dishes.*
>
> —AGATHA CHRISTIE
> English writer of detective fiction

Select one intense experience from your list to write about today, and then place this list of subjects in your greenhouse folder.

Now you are ready you to use the technique that follows whenever you want to convey an experience to readers so they will live it with you.

To brainstorm through your five senses to help your readers internalize your chosen experience, do the following:

Write your name in the center of an $8\frac{1}{2} \times 11$-inch or larger sheet of paper.

Think of a particular moment in the experience you're about to describe. Then, in your mind, locate yourself in the precise spot where you were. With pen poised, imagine that your page is an overview of the setting, with yourself in the center where your name is written, and proceed to name everything you remember seeing.

First, use your sense of vision. Write the names of things you see from your location. Place the names of the things you can touch close to your name in the center of

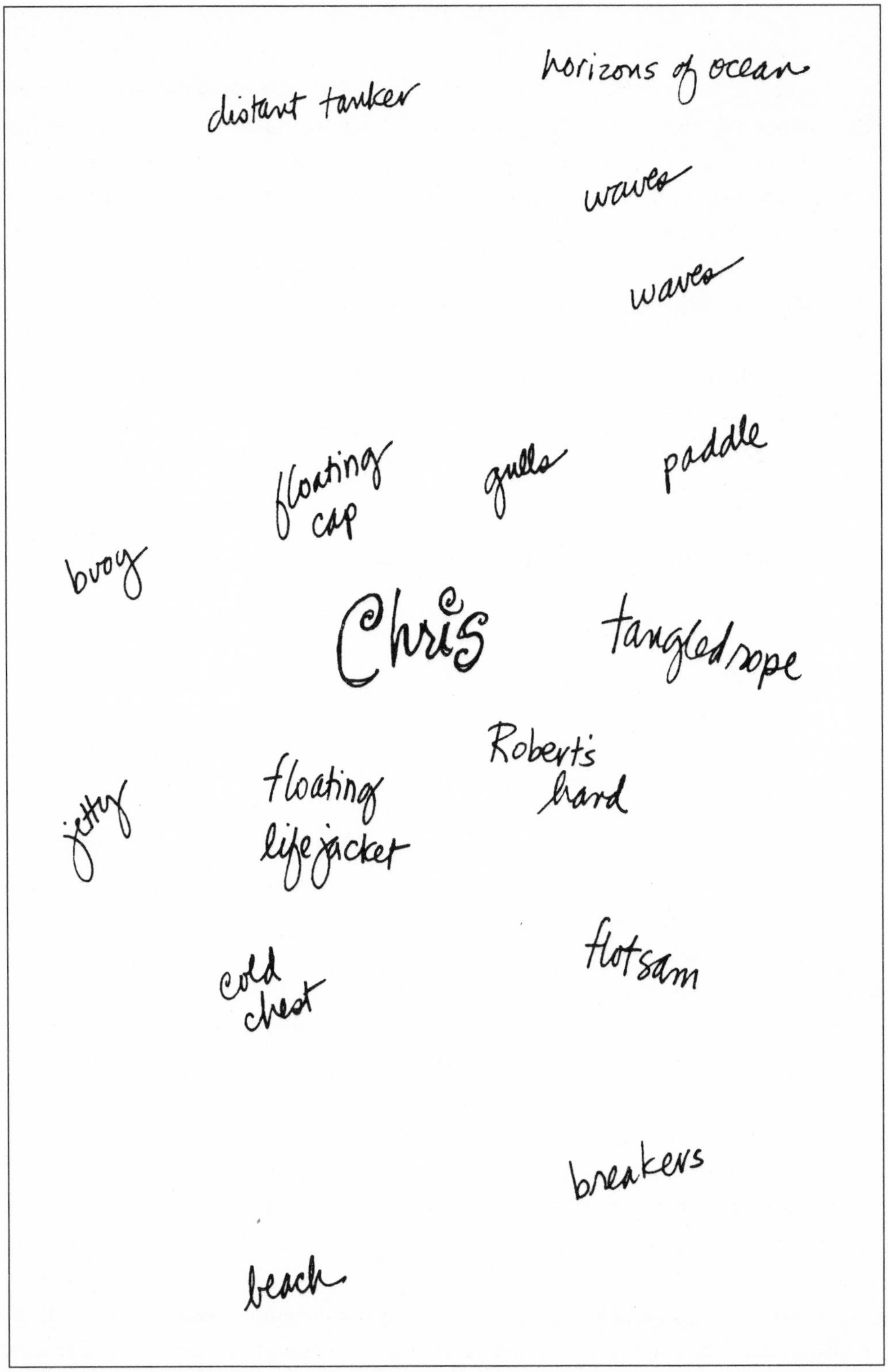

distant tanker

horizons of ocean

waves

waves

floating cap

gulls

paddle

buoy

Chris

tangled rope

Robert's hard

jetty

floating life jacket

cold chest

flotsam

breakers

beach

Figure 3

the paper. Place the distant objects out near the edges of the paper. Name everything you remember seeing. (See figure 3.)

Next, name the sounds you heard. Write the names of nearby sounds close to your name and the names of distant, background sounds near the edges of the paper. Write in larger letters any predominant sounds or sounds that startled you. If someone spoke, record the person's words inside of quotation marks. If you said something, quote yourself.

Your paper is now becoming spattered with words. The more crowded it becomes, the more material you'll have at your disposal. So far you've analyzed only sight and sound; as you continue brainstorming through your senses, your page will become crammed with words. Not all of the following suggestions will apply to your experience, so just pass over those that don't work. Suggestions that don't fit this subject may work well with your next subject.

The sense of touch covers a broad range of feelings. Near the center of the page, name objects you actually were touching.

- Name what you were wearing.
- Tell how your body felt.
    ~ Which muscles were taut?
    ~ What was your posture like?
    ~ What were your hands doing?
    ~ How did your throat feel?
    ~ How did you hold your mouth (move your eyes, breathe)?
- Describe the atmosphere.
    ~ What was the temperature?
    ~ Where was the source of light? Describe its quality.
    ~ What were the shadows like?
    ~ How did the air feel? Compare the air to music.
- What was the predominant color in this scene?
- Tell how you felt about what was happening.
- Name your mood. What was its flavor and color?
- What rhythm describes your feelings?
- Think about the smells in the background of your experience. Name them.
- How did the objects near you smell?
- How did the people smell? Include yourself.
- What odors were produced by something happening?
- Name wafting scents.

If you had a taste or flavor in your mouth, name it. A young man writing about a diving experience mentioned the salty taste of ocean water in his mouth. Taste may or may not be a part of your remembered experience.

You can use this technique of brainstorming through your five senses anytime you want to write an account so that it will give a sense of presence to your readers. All you need is a large sheet of paper. Remembering your experience, locate yourself in a certain moment and in a certain place. Then, using your five senses, write words that describe your perceptions. You'll be aware of and use many of them when you begin writing.

The function of language is not to inform but to evoke.
What I seek in speech is the response of the other.

—JACQUES LACAN
French psychoanalyst

At this time you have identified an experience to narrate, and now you have a page showing many sensory details that you can include in your account. You probably won't include all the sensations on this page, and you may add other ideas. The brainstorming page just provides a systematic scheme to give you a wealth of specific, vivid material with which to begin writing.

Place your brainstorming page of ideas in a spot where you can see it as you write your rough draft. One good way to begin is: "When I was..." This phrase will help orient readers regarding your age or the stage of your life at the time of the experience. If location is relevant, tell where you were. Like a news reporter, include when and where, and then proceed to tell why and how.

Bonnie Gundeloch Johnson, a psychiatric nurse who has worked closely with elderly and dying patients, wrote the following account after identifying a significant experience in her life and then naming her perceptions at the time. Her description is vivid because she systematically reminded herself of her sensations.

Night Trip to Eugene

The experience was part of my awakening. The summer air in hushed sounds rushing past the car under the summer sky. Dark hills to the left, black-and-gray fields in crisscross patterns to the right. My foot on the accelerator, my car traveling the gray strip of highway. Faint sounds trickled from the radio. The dashboard light illuminated the car. My white Australian shepherd dog curled on the seat next to me. I drove on and on from Seattle to Eugene with a two-hour stop in Washougal,

Washington, for a stress-filled meeting with my soon-to-be ex-husband about division of the property.

I left at dusk, when the last embers of pink and yellow were fading from the western horizon. Crossing the expansive 205 bridge to Portland, getting gas from an overly cheerful attendant with hair in a dark ponytail down his back. Feeling patronized. Then emerging from the lights of Portland into the dark stretches of open country.

I should stop. I am becoming very tired. I should eat something. I should rest.

Voices in my head. Feeling free. So this is what it is like. Am I free now? Feels free. Feels independent. I feel happy! I should stop. Eyes closing. Oops. Keep eyes open. Very tired. Very tired.

Car ahead, I am rapidly approaching. Foot on brake. Lucky. Darkness. Wake up! Sing. Sing loud! Drive… drive. Eyes hurt. Glare. Put on sunglasses. Comfort. Tired. Should stop, should stop. Eyelids closing over parched eyeballs. Open. Please stay open. Open! So tired. Need to rest just a few seconds. Keep driving. Help. Tail-lights coming up—slow car. Help! Brake! Lost control. Swerve to left. Hit car. Propelled car off the road. Hit car! Something flipping over in midair. Crashing down. Rolling. Smoking. Rolling. What have I done!

Quiet.

Read your description aloud slowly. Savor every word. Listen with your eyes half shut as if someone were reading a novel to you. Inhale its vapors.

If you are writing in a gathering of writers, form larger response groups this time because this draft is one you'll especially enjoy hearing. Of course, you'll:

- Suspend judgment.
- Size your feet to fit the writer's boots.
- Remain mum about what you'll hear.

Respond by remarking on what, in your own mind, you see, hear, feel, smell, and taste. And if you are acutely curious about something, ask a question.

When you reflect on the draft you've written, take detailed notes in response to the following questions, which may cause you to ponder. Your notes are likely to develop into ideas you'll insert into your draft.

- What did the experience mean to you at the time?
- Why did you choose to explore this subject now?
- How does the experience fit into your life?
- Within the experience, are there any instances of tenderness (grace, compassion, mercy)?

Revise your draft. Expand it. Cross out whatever didn't work as you intended. Change words or phrases. Rearrange paragraphs any way you wish. A well-revised draft is sometimes so covered with marks that it's almost unintelligible.

When your draft sounds right, then have it proofread. The amount of proofreading your draft needs depends on your plans for it. If you're going to give copies to only the members of your immediate family and your close friends, then you probably don't need to have it checked for grammar and usage. These people will like "hearing" you write the way you talk.

If you like to sketch, consider illustrating your final version. Insert any photographs and clippings or documents you may have. Those pictures and other items will be preserved when you make copies of your final version on acid-free paper.

As an experiment, use the brainstorming technique you learned in this chapter on the subject you wrote about for your warm-up writing. Then see how the two rough drafts differ.

The more aware you are of the sensory aspects of your life, the more effectively you will be able to employ the brainstorming technique. At times when you do rote tasks or when you are inactive, take stock of all sensory perceptions. While sitting in a waiting room, brushing your teeth, watching soccer practice, riding the bus, or raking leaves, systematically ask yourself, "What do I see, hear, smell, feel, and taste?" Observe both close range and distant perceptions. Notice your posture, your breathing, and which muscles are tense. Analyze your mood. By increasing your awareness of these sensory aspects of your life, you will not only gain skill as a writer but also deepen your appreciation of your life.

> *Eternal One, Sovereign God of the universe:*
> *You remove sleep from the eyes, slumber from the eyelids.*
> *Help me to be awake this day to the wonders that surround me,*
> *alive to beauty and love and aware that all being is precious,*
> *that wherever we go, we walk on holy ground.*
>   —Traditional Jewish prayer for the morning

CHAPTER 5

Internalized Places

Religious awe is the same organic thrill
which we feel in a forest at twilight, or in a mountain gorge.

—WILLIAM JAMES
American philosopher and psychologist

WE CARRY A LANDSCAPE within us. The places where we have lived, worked, and felt sharp emotions continue to reside in our being as part of us. These places can be retrieved through subtle, sensuous associations that summon an entire scene. Unexpected stimuli—particular smells, light at a certain slant, a distant sound, the taste and texture of a food from our youth—can draw us back in time.

The French author of *Remembrance of Things Past*, Marcel Proust, reflected on his retrieved memory of a childhood place, brought about by the flavor of a little cake, a petite madeleine.

> *And suddenly the memory returns. The taste was that of the little crumb of madeleine which on Sunday mornings at Combray (because on those mornings I did not go out before church-time), when I went to say good day to her in her bedroom, my aunt Léonie used to give me, dipping it first in her own cup of real or of lime-flower tea…when from a long-distant past nothing subsists, after the people are dead, after the things are broken and scattered, still, alone, more fragile, but with more vitality, more unsubstantial, more persistent, more faithful, the smell and taste of things remain poised long time, like souls, ready to remind us, waiting and hoping for their moment, amid the ruins of all the rest; and bear unfaltering, in the tiny and almost impalpable drop of their essence, the vast structure of recollection.*

It was the smell and taste of the tea-soaked madeleine that retrieved memories of an old gray house, streets along which he ran errands, country roads, M. Swann's park. *"And the whole of Combray and of its surroundings, taking their proper shapes and growing solid, sprang into being, town and gardens alike, from my cup of tea."*

Our senses both evoke memories in ourselves and, when included in our descriptive writing, convey a sense of presence. This chapter will guide you in using your senses as you describe a place, applying the technique introduced in chapter 4. But first, help your words begin to flow with a quick write.

Rapidly write a description of any place you recall vividly. Your choice of subjects could range from your grandmother's kitchen to a worksite, a campsite, or a cathedral; think of any place that has impressed itself on your being. The place may have been nurturing or loathsome. Limit the scope of your description to your visual range from an exact spot.

This quick rough draft will be like a still-life taken from the flow of your retrieved memories. At this time you will set the scene. The description may turn out to be one you'll develop later by telling about yourself when you were there.

To initiate the flow of words, use any of the following prompts or make up one of your own. Then, using any subject that comes to mind, write rapidly and impulsively. Unplanned writing can be startlingly insightful.

- A place I remember well is…
- I could hardly wait to get out of…
- I would like to return to…

The following excerpt is from the memoirs of Richard Colley, a cashier at Wal-Mart and a creator of fractal image designs for large latch-hook rugs. He recalls visiting the site of his elementary school in Wilder, Idaho.

The flagpole rose up out of a cement walkway, pointlessly connecting the front steps to the unbusy highway. No longer did Old Glory ruffle its canvas or snap a trusty acknowledgment to the wind. The southward vestige was merely the soft clacking of the flag's chain in the midsummer wind.

Near the northeast corner of the building is a sturdy merry-go-round. I remember making it spin around wildly and then riding it until I was dizzy. My pals and I got it moving around and we played "chicken." The object was to see who could stay on the longest before leaping off. We boys tolerated that play until we were nauseous.

The brick schoolhouse had three levels: basement, ground level, and upper level. Being in fifth grade was special because townspeople said the building was a "fire trap." The fifth-grade classroom was on the upper level. A window on the west side opened onto the landing of a fire escape. Its special attraction was the long slide that fifth graders could go down during fire drills. The walls of the slide were high with smooth, rounded "arms." The official policy was not to play on the fire escape slide, but many of the more adventurous boys, and occasional tomboys, were wont to break the rule.

This description portrays not only a bleak brick school but also a place where growing children spun all possible amusement from a merry-go-round and exploited the off-limits thrill of climbing up and whooshing down an outdoor fire escape.

To hear your own description if you're writing independently:

- Set your draft aside for a day. Don't read it aloud to yourself until tomorrow. This interim will distance you from it and lend perspective so you can hear it anew.
- Ask a close friend to listen to your draft and then name its strengths and ask a question about something not told.
- Tape-record your draft, and then listen to it as if it were written by someone else—preferably a good friend whose feelings you respect.

If you're writing with a group of writers, follow the aforementioned guidelines for good listening, and respond in the recommended ways.

Should you decide to expand and develop the description you've just written, and you want to give readers a vivid sense of place, add information about the impressions your five senses consciously, or subliminally, perceived. We usually do describe what we see, but we often forget to use our other senses. Read through your narrative, watching for places where you can add descriptions of:

- Sounds
  - ~ Background sounds
  - ~ Human sounds
  - ~ Sounds resulting from actions
- Touch
  - ~ Surfaces with which you came into contact
  - ~ The way your body felt
  - ~ The atmosphere around you
- Smells
- Tastes

In addition to describing sensory impressions, tell what you felt and thought.

Here are remembrances of two different kitchens. The use of sensory description by both writers gives us a feel for each place.

This description is from Rosemary Batori's memoirs. She lived in England until a handsome American soldier arrived during World War II, courted her, married her, and brought her to his home in Oregon. Notice Rosemary's use of smell.

North Wootton Farm, Nr. Sherborne, Dorset

> *Breakfast was always served in the enormous, stone-floored kitchen, with Aunt Mae, our stepgrandmother, moving back and forth to the attached dairy room, supervising the dairymaids at their work of separating the milk and churning the butter.*
>
> *The kitchen opened onto the farmyard. Any time the door opened, sounds and smells were wafted into the kitchen—the rotting hay, horse and cow manure—an aroma with little appeal to townsfolk but nostalgically attractive to a farmer's granddaughter.*

The kitchens of grandmothers seem to be fondly remembered by many memoirists, even though the smells made their noses tickle.

Jean Clark remembered a time when she and her cousin Roberta, ages five and seven, stayed at their Grandmother Robertson's farm for a few days. Grandmother Robertson taught the girls how to make butter by churning with a broom handle attached to a round wooden dowel.

> *That kitchen was a cozy place. A fire was going in the stove, warming the entire kitchen. Every now and then Grandmother would lift the lid on top of the stove and poke in another stick of wood, at the same time stirring up the fire with a poker sending a shower of sparks into the air. The smell of sour milk and burning wood tickled our noses. The yeasty aroma of bread rising on top of the warming oven filled the air.*
>
> *Splish! Splash! went the broom handle up and down in the crock. "When will it be done?" we kept asking. Arms were beginning to feel tired. Every now and then Grandmother would stop her bread making, giving the handle a brisk, firm chug, chug, and offering words of encouragement. "It's almost done."*

Jean not only used the senses of smell, sound, and feeling but she also included quotations, another effective technique.

You're now ready to write a rough draft for a second description. First gather ideas. On a sheet of notebook paper, name places that you have strong feelings about.

- A safe and happy place in your childhood
- A place where you felt helpless and afraid
- The place where you went to be alone
- Your favorite place as a teenager
- A place where you learned or discovered something
- A place where something embarrassing happened
- A place where something frightening happened
- A place where you had an encounter with another person
- Your first job site
- A place where you felt in jeopardy or threatened
- A place where you were given medical treatment
- Your place of worship, meditation, or repose
- The location of an important ceremony
- A place you created for yourself or your family
- A place where you received bad or good news
- A place where you excelled
- A place where you were defeated
- A place where you were intimate with someone
- The location of a fight
- A place of birth or death
- A restorative place where you felt relaxed and calm

From among your many subjects, pick the place you'd like to write about today. Then store your list of ideas for further descriptions in your greenhouse file.

Use a fresh sheet of paper to prepare to write a description of an internalized place. Following the technique presented in chapter 4, write your name in the center of the page. Imagine that you are in the center of the page and that the paper is the place you are going to describe. Travel mentally to the place you'll describe and locate yourself in a particular spot.

First, write the names of things you see as you look out from your position. Name those in the foreground and the background. What colors are they? Be precise. Name exact shades. Include shadows and darkness, as well as details that stand out.

Next, remember and name the sounds in your place. Think of the natural sounds in addition to noises made by machinery and by people. Write down sentences spoken by yourself and others. Include faraway sounds. If the place is quiet, describe its quietness. Someone climbing above the timberline on Mount Audubon might hear only the rustle of her own parka blown by the wind, her individual breaths, boots against rock, and the occasional shriek of a marmot.

Moving on, address the sense of touch—the feel of objects you are touching or the feel of the equipment you are using, the feel and texture of your clothing, the way your body feels. Write words descriptive of the textures of things around you. How would you describe the atmosphere (temperature, humidity)? What words describe the mood of the place? What is your own mood?

Now describe the tastes and smells of your place, which are interrelated. If something is in your mouth, tell how it tastes, but give more attention to smells. Name the nearby odors and then the smells airborne from farther away. Include your own scent as well as that of other people and animals.

Lilly Burgard described her feelings about arriving at a reservoir in the Cascade Mountains as the sun was sinking. This is the first paragraph of a chapter entitled "The Reservoir."

> *I looked out the window, and the light swirled and shifted, entered my eyes and traveled down my throat, making my solar plexus tingle and burn. "Let's go out in the boat," I suggested. The evening held a unique beauty. It was Indian summer and a full moon was due to rise within the hour. There was a smell in the air, so sweet I knew the night had potential for magic.*

Lilly takes us beyond the world of physics when she writes, "the light swirled and shifted, entered my eyes and traveled down my throat, making my solar plexus tingle and burn." We know we're in for an interesting boat ride.

The rough draft you'll now write should be sloppy because it is hurriedly composed. Scan your page of notes for ideas, but do not be limited to them. They serve only as a reference for including sensory description as you tell about the place. As you write, allow the feeling of the place to guide you wherever it goes.

Next, listen to your draft read aloud, and if possible consider any response. This important step should never be skipped. Your editing will be far more effective if you've heard your draft read aloud and better yet if you've also heard responses from listeners. Follow the guidelines you've learned for listening and responding.

When you are ready to reflect on this description of a place, take time to jot notes on another sheet of paper in response to the following questions:

- Why is the place you chose meaningful to you?
- What does your chosen place show about your values and about yourself?
- Does the place in some way take you beyond your usual self?
- How would you be different if you had not known this place?
- When do you think of the place, and how do you feel when you remember it?

Now look at the notes you've taken and then reread your rough draft. Would integration of your notes into your rough draft give it more depth?

Revise your draft, proofread it, give it a title, and write your final version. If you're writing by hand and make minor errors, just draw neat lines through them and continue. Corrections are not offensive.

It's possible that some descriptions appearing in the final draft will reflect awe, wonder, reverence, contentment, or joy. Sacredness can occur in improbable places. Equally significant, the absence of those qualities may reveal longing in the soul of the writer.

In her writings about her childhood in eastern Oregon during World War II, novelist Debra Burgess-Mohr captured wonderings about hatred and beauty. Notice that the first paragraph gives the flavor of the historical period, while the second paragraph pinpoints a series of moments in a particular place.

It seemed that an extraordinary number of young boys, sons of friends of my parents, were called up in the draft or had enlisted. My mother rolled bandages down at the city hall; my father, who was in the army during World War I, was in some sort of volunteer group that watched the skies at night for enemy planes. Food—sugar, butter, flour, and meat-—was rationed; gasoline was allocated according to profession. "A" cards went to doctors and farmers, "B" cards were issued to men like my father, and "C" cards were available for the rest.

At night German prisoners of war, who had been brought to our county to work the farms and ranches, worked in the pea cannery in our town. Often, late at night,

I awoke to hear them singing in the trucks that brought them into town and transported them back to the barracks behind barbed fences not far from Pendleton. I was amazed at the beauty of their songs and wondered how I could hate someone who made such beautiful music.

The Soul of a Child

In every child who is born, under no matter what circumstances,
and of no matter what parents, the potentiality of the human race
is born again; and in him, too, once more, and of each of us,
our terrific responsibility towards human life; towards
the utmost idea of goodness, of the horror of error, and of God.

—JAMES AGEE
American journalist, social critic, poet, and novelist

IN WRITING THIS chapter of your memoirs you'll give glimpses of a tender part of yourself, your inner life when you were small. You'll show your relationship with members of your family and community, in addition to showing your young self.

Begin with a warm-up writing.

Rouse your fluency by first scrawling a quick, careless rough draft. This time, consider writing in response to more than one of the following prompts. You may change the phrasing of any of them or write about a different subject you remember as important in your childhood.

- My mother (father, other relative) used to always say…
- A game I played involved…(Tell about the invisible, as well as the visible.)
- In my childhood I was most afraid of…
- I'm like my mother (father, other relative) in these ways…—and different in these ways…
- The person I wanted to be like was…
- The way I fit (didn't fit) into my family was…

An especially good way to hear your rough draft is to give it to someone who will read it to you. Sit back and listen to it as if it were written by a stranger. Interrupt the reader whenever you want to write notes in the margins as reminders of changes you would like to make.

> If you listen to the accounts of fellow writers, remember to remain nonjudgmental and confidential about their readings, and respond by first pointing out what you admire about the writing. After that, ask a question.

Over the years, Sara Schwake has worked as a medical assistant and in clerical support positions; currently she works for Head Start. She says she "gleans plenty of memoir material" from the tales her two sons tell of their childhood, as well as from her own youth.

Sara wrote about an unexpected and unwelcome appearance her father made at the elementary school she attended. Notice how the specific details she gave enable us to picture her father. We see also how Sara felt about him and about herself.

> *A time when I did not feel in control was when my father unexpectedly, and without welcome, appeared in the hall outside my third-grade classroom. There he was—all 6'4" of him, looking as animated as he always could during a manic phase—his wide, goofy smile showing decaying teeth. He didn't care! There he was trying to belong to those traditional wide, shining wooden hallways seemingly filled with young faces staring up at this grinning and gangly man. I would believe that I tried, out of my shock and chagrin, to disappear back into my classroom instead of leaving for a carefree recess. Did my stern, spinster teacher offer me some protection by not letting him know where I was? I couldn't tolerate the link that might be made between me, this growing-into-gangly young girl, and this man who wanted to talk to anyone who'd listen to his often disconnected yet constant ramblings. My mom would have been at work and unaware of his likely bored escape and his subsequent foray into a place I had always, until then, felt safe from the havoc he could create. But in truth, I don't remember any other such unwelcome visits. So, out there in words I didn't hear, I think an adult sensed how small I felt and shielded me.*

Did you notice that Sara used the adjective "gangly" to describe both her father and herself? Sara's quick warm-up writing allowed repetition of a word that reveals her subconscious fear of being associated with her father.

Now you are ready to capture ideas for a second subject. On a sheet of paper draw an overview map showing an approximate blueprint of either your childhood home or the home in which you spent the most memorable part of your childhood. Leave room around the outside walls of the building for the yard or street. Your blueprint need not be drawn to scale or even accurate. Distortions and omissions will indicate your perception of your home when you were very young.

In the place where you slept, draw a rectangle for your bed. In the place where you ate, draw an overhead view of the table and chairs. Write the letter *P* where you played indoors. Outside the walls of the structure indicate trees or shrubs you remember and any outbuildings or other features. Write the letter *P* where you played outdoors. If you can remember names for the following, write them along the margin of the page:

- The street or road that passed your home
- Neighbors
- Playmates
- Pets or farm animals

Look at your blueprint and write the letter *G* where something good happened. Write the letter *B* where something bad happened. Write the letter *T* for "talk" where someone said something that you remember. (See figure 4.)

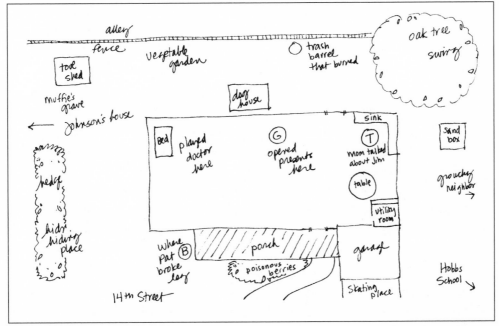

Figure 4

Find a partner or friend who will listen while you explain your blueprint. Point to and tell about everything you've drawn and about things you haven't drawn. Your account will reach into receded memories, so explain everything you can. Let your blueprint serve as a catalyst for recovering forgotten parts of your childhood.

> If you are writing with a partner, listen while she explains her blueprint.

Write a quick, error-strewn draft about any incident you remember from your childhood, or describe a typical event. Think about what you did on weekends. Remember something that happened at school. What special occasion did you eagerly anticipate? Did it turn out the way you expected? You might write about the first time you did something—your first day at school, your first time away from home, the first time you played a sport or were in a performance.

We have romanticized childhood as a time of innocence, and it is. Ironically, however, cruelty resides within the innocent nature of the child. We are first aware of cruelty when we are its victims; we arrive at a higher level of awareness when we recognize ourselves as its perpetrators.

The following excerpt is from the memoirs of Kirsten Jones, an arts consultant and grant writer. Born a first-generation American in San Francisco, she moved to Oregon in search of a more meaningful life.

> *I remember playing with a gang of neighborhood children only once. I was about nine and probably hadn't lived in that house too long— don't think I even knew the children's names. I must have known them enough to join in, but I have no other memories of them.*
>
> *Somehow on this particular day, I got to be the leader. How did that happen? We raced up and down the street, shrieking away. As a mob, without any planning or forethought we started chasing the girl who lived next door to me. I remember the "rush" of being on the attack, of being stronger, of having numbers behind me. We caught her, and she and I had a fight. She pulled my hair really hard, and I pulled hers. I got her down on the ground and sat astride her. In the flush of victory, our eyes locked, and I had no idea what to do next. I began to feel embarrassed, uncomfortable, ashamed. Can't remember what the rest of gang wanted.*

The girl wanted to go home, and she promised to come back out after she was cleaned up. Surprisingly, we allowed it and waited. Equally surprising, she came out again and all awkwardly gathered around and said something—can't remember what. I'm sure that by that time, none of us was happy about how things had turned out. I remember the feeling of respect I had for this girl after she came out and my regret for my actions.

I have no memory of seeing her again. My mother was in bed with a bad back, and my stepfather was overseas. She sold the house soon after, and we moved to Germany.

During my adult life, whenever I've heard of mob actions I remember that day and how I felt. I remember the feeling of power and I remember the shame. I understand how mobs get out of control—and I've stayed far away.

You might again ask someone to read your draft to you so you can listen to it.

If you're writing independently, listen to your own oral reading and then decide what aspect of your writing seems strongest. Ask yourself what questions would occur to a stranger who heard it.

When we hear our early drafts, we often decide to edit them. We may add information, change the way we said something, rearrange paragraphs and sentences, or even cut parts out.

Consider adding sensory description. You may still remember particular smells, tastes, sounds, or the feel of something you touched. It's not necessary to use all five senses; even a few will render your writing more vivid.

If you remember what someone said, quote that person.

After you've listened to a reading of your rough draft and made the changes your ear told you to make, then reflect on the deeper meanings within your writing. Write sentences or paragraphs in response to the following questions. When you see how you've answered them, you may discover information to add to your rough draft.

- What was your source of childhood security?
- Whom did you love most?
- What kinds of experiences distressed you?
- Were you aware of a child who was picked on? If so, what were your feelings at the time?
- Explain how you do, or do not, see your childhood as a time of innocence.
- How was harmony created or shattered in your childhood?
- How did you overcome your childhood fears?
- In retrospect, what strengths emerged from within you?

When you have revised your rough draft as much as you wish, then give it a title, proofread it, and write a final version. Arrange the page with space for photographs of yourself as a child. Be sure to write a caption under each one. If you enjoy drawing, illustrate this chapter with sketches of your pets, favorite toys, and the places where you played.

Father Theodore Berktold, an Episcopal rector in Eugene, Oregon, wrote about his childhood in Minnesota where his Roman Catholic family lived on a farm. You will see his relationship to his parents and siblings.

My mom would drive into town from our farm on Saturday afternoons and go to confession, dropping some of her nine children off at my grandparents' home one block from the church. I was a quiet and well-behaved child (being older), so I went along with her to church. She always had a baby in her arms. I sat through confession in the pews, and then went into the baptistery with her to light a candle and pray silently. I would get to drop the nickel in the slot of the long brass tube, old and well polished, where the change collected. We would spend what seemed like a long time there (it was probably brief) and she would take me by the hand and carry the youngest child back down the street to my grandparents. We would have a cup of coffee with my grandmother, then drive back to the farm.

Saturday morning was washday for her, rolling out the washing machine and stands and tubs, heating water in the reservoir of the wood-fired stove, and filling the washing machine with a dipping can. She would wash whites and dress clothes first, ending with muddy clothes (overalls). Saturday supper was always a good meal, because Sunday was a fast day until we had gone to communion. Seated around the table, we would always pray the same words together, hands folded and heads bowed: "Bless us, O Lord, and these thy gifts we are about to receive from thy bounty, through Christ our Lord, Amen." Saturday evening was a time for us all to take a bath in the same clothes washtubs placed on the floor in front of the wood stove (the oven door open in winter to keep us warm), girls going first (they were cleaner) and boys last, using a bar of homemade soap of lye and tallow. We baked it in a cake pan when we were butchering over Christmas vacation, then cut and stacked it like brownies for later use. After baths, with everyone in pajamas we would kneel together in the living/dining room and pray the rosary together, pulling chairs out from the table, leaning on the seats and facing the backs of the chairs. As I got older, I would often lead the rosary. Then we would sit together facing the black-and-white TV on the small table in the corner of the room, Dad would adjust the picture, make popcorn on the wood stove. I would turn the crank to keep a curved wire scraping the bottom of the pot to prevent burned kernels in the hot lard, again produced from our butchering, popping corn we had grown and stored in whole ears under my bed next to the walnuts because my bedroom was above the kitchen and had a dry floor from the heat of the stove. When Gunsmoke *was over, the TV went off, Mom lit a vigil light in front of a picture of Mary, and the older kids went upstairs to bed; Mary Ann and Peggy to the left, Ted and Joe to the right, past the toilet mounted in a widened area of the hallway of the ancient farmhouse. We would all brush our teeth and get the popcorn shells out, pee, and fall asleep looking at the frost designs on the window reflected in the brightness of a winter moon.*

People Who Etched an Imprint

Whenever two people meet there are really six people present.
There is each man as he sees himself, each man as the other person sees him,
and each man as he really is.

—WILLIAM JAMES
American philosopher and psychologist

THE PEOPLE WE remember, beginning with those who tended us when we were very young and continuing to our present companions and associates, have influenced our assessment of all humankind and of ourselves. Those people are the framework upon which we wove bonds of trust, evolved a sense of self-worth, and learned to work cooperatively and share pleasures. From negative people we learn to be mistrustful and to doubt our own value. This chapter will help you identify key people in your life, write about them and the ways in which they influenced you, and recognize the part of you that responded to them.

To find your fluency, scrawl a fast first draft. Make up your own prompt or choose one of the following:

- The person I have felt happiest being with is…
- Someone who made a period in my life miserable was…
- If I could again be with someone from my past, it would be…because…

After you've written your rough draft, read it to a sensitive listener or a small critiquing group—or read it aloud to yourself. If you are writing independently, take the draft through the remaining steps of the writing process. If you are writing with colleagues, however, set your rough draft aside to complete later.

To begin your next chapter, first gather ideas. On a sheet of notebook paper, draw rows of oval or square picture frames that are each large enough to accommodate the name of a person. Your gallery of frames may consist simply of ovals or squares, or you may draw ornate frames. Toward the end of this chapter, you'll use your gallery in another way, for which you'll need the rows of frames.

Inside each frame, write the name of the person who occurs to you. It's all right if you list the same name repeatedly, and you may name more than one person in each category. Write the first names that come to mind.

Name someone who has:

- Given comfort
- Caused distress
- Guided you
- Befriended you
- Elicited desire
- Made demands
- Received your care
- Caused grief
- Stifled you
- Encouraged you
- Sparked fun
- Been dependable
- Taken care of you
- Shaped your beliefs
- Raised doubts
- Energized you
- Stimulated curiosity
- Stoked creativity
- Brought out your best
- Brought out your worst
- Taught you
- Taught you an important lesson

From your list, choose one person as your subject. The person about whom your feelings, positive or negative, are strongest would be a good choice. After you have chosen your subject, file this list of ideas in your greenhouse folder for future writings.

Next, write your chosen subject's name in the center of a blank page. You're going to jot brief notes on this page that may not make sense to anyone but yourself. Your scribblings will revive memories and enable you to include details you might otherwise ignore.

Close your eyes halfway and visualize your subject.

Remember your subject's physical characteristics. Write words that describe the person's stature, posture, way of walking and moving the body, and any habitual gestures.

Visualize the skin. Imagine touching it. Imagine touching the face. Describe any makeup. How are the teeth?

How would the hair feel? What is its color?

Remember the hands. What is the condition of the nails?

What does the subject tend to wear? What sort of shoes, glasses, jewelry.

How would you describe the voice? Can you remember a typical sentence or phrase? If so, write it down. How did the subject usually breathe?

What smells do you associate with the subject?

Moving from physical characteristics to traits and personality, ask yourself what the subject most enjoyed. What made the person happy? Angry? Weary? Name the person's goals and concerns. What is your subject's predominant mood? What color do you associate with your subject?

If you were going to liken your subject to an animal, which animal would you choose? If to weather, what sort of weather? If to music, what category of music? If to a vehicle, what kind of vehicle? What type of plant does your subject suggest? A cactus? A vine?

You now have more notes than you're likely to use, but you have brought to mind many observations to help describe your subject. The following prompts are ways to begin this draft:

- Someone who…
- I will never forget…

> *If you cannot get rid of the family skeleton,*
> *you may as well make it dance.*

—GEORGE BERNARD SHAW
Irish playwright, critic, and novelist

Lowell Andrew Thomas chose to describe his grandmother. The scene is set in Mississippi, where he spent his early life. He and his wife, Peggy, now live in Oregon.

Someone who meant a lot to me was my granny. When I was born, she was seventy-three and had failing eyesight that eventually left her blind. Some memories:

- *That she was stooped and skinny with dark Cherokee skin and didn't talk much except to me.*
- *Drying watermelon seeds and putting them into little cotton bags with drawstrings while listening to Granny tell me how they would turn into watermelons again after we planted them in the spring.*
- *Sitting before the fireplace in a room with unpainted wooden walls that were lit by kerosene lamps.*
- *Getting off the school bus one day and being attacked by a guinea that had her nest in a roadside ditch. As I ran across the yard screaming, the guinea on top of my head clawing my scalp, I saw Granny run from the house and sprint across the yard with her homemade broom. I was so surprised to see that she could run that I almost forgot my pain and terror.*
- *How carefully she kept her yard swept and how refreshing it felt to lie upon the naked earth on a hot day.*
- *After my family moved to town, going to the store on my bicycle to buy snuff for Granny. She liked Levi Garrett. It came in little cans: the plain flavor had a white label, and the scotch flavor had an orange label. Each came with a flat wooden spoon for dipping.*
- *Granny sitting in her chair the last few years of her life rocking back and forth slowly all day long. How her room during those years was in back of the house, away from the rest of the family.*
- *Listening to Granny tell about being an orphan who was taken in by a family named Grey and how the Greys often had company for days at a time and held dances at their house.*
- *How I had a fight with Granny one day and said mean things and how shocked and sorry I was when she cried like a little girl.*
- *Running in from playing one day to find Granny sitting on the floor in the back of the long dark hallway. I nearly laughed to see her there until she called to me in pain from a broken hip.*
- *Going to her funeral and not crying and being praised by my father for acting like a man.*
- *That she said she loved me more than she had ever loved anyone or anything.*

To revise your draft, make any changes you wish. Check to see if you described your subject's appearance and personality, and told how the person affected you. Freely insert this and other information.

In the following excerpt from her memoirs, Adrienne Lannom shows how her grandmother affected her.

I don't remember that she ever said to me, "I love you." It sort of came out of her like waves washing over me. Now that I've just written that, I recognize the pull the ocean has for me—the sense of homecoming, the laying down of cares and burdens, the long ecstatic intake of breath and the ocean smell filling me.

Grandma had a special smell that was unlike any other I've experienced since my first and last memories of her. I think it was a combination of baking and cooking smells, especially bread-making smells, and the scent of a lotion she ritually applied every night after unpinning and brushing her hair. She wasn't a Norman Rockwell picture-book grandmother, although she was tiny and round and sturdy. The bread she took from the oven often failed to rise, sat heavily on the table, and tasted deliciously of failed yeast. It was a visible sign of her love and was always there for me when I came to visit.

Grandma never instructed or corrected. There was nothing I did that went unaffirmed. I was wonderful in her sight, and everything I did was also—being a crepe-paper jonquil in a nursery school pageant, playing in my first piano recital, winning a third-grade spelling bee, introducing her to my first real boyfriend, running up the four half-flights of stairs to her apartment after she pressed the buzzer that let me push open the heavy downstairs door, and hugging her.

And I knew myself to be a different person with her—a better person. For her, I wanted to be perfect, doing all the things my parents struggled in vain to get me to do at home. So it was that after I became a parent and my children grew up and went away, I couldn't wait to become a grandparent. I thought they'd never get married, and then I wondered if they'd ever have children. I should have trusted that love like Grandma's couldn't be denied and that it goes on through me to each one of my grandchildren and will, through them, to theirs.

Consider whether your subject embodies any of the following qualities or stimulates them in yourself.

- Generosity
- Devotion
- Mercy
- Compassion

If you can remember the words someone spoke, even approximately, put quotation marks around them and include them in your narration. Write your own spoken responses in the same way. Dialogue gives a sense of drama and immediacy to writing. Imagine what the last novel you read would be like without dialogue.

Enjoy revising this draft.

You have written a gift. If you wrote about someone you admire or love, consider making a copy of your description to give to that person. A workshop participant who wrote about her deceased sister could not give her writing to her sister, so she made copies for her sister's children. As Thanksgiving approached, she mailed them out as a celebration and offering of thanks for their mother.

One of my college students, a young man who had written an admiring description of his hardworking, single mother, gave it to her on her birthday. The next time our class met, he told me it brought tears to her eyes. An attractive way to present your description as a gift is to roll it like a scroll and tie a ribbon around it. A red ribbon around your scroll makes a memorable valentine present.

> *For love is an attitude toward reality*
> *usually of someone finite toward something infinite.*
>
> —JOSEPH BRODSKY
> U.S. Poet Laureate, 1991–1992

If you are imaginative, experiment using the following suggestion. Take your gallery of "portraits" from your greenhouse folder. Squint at the picture frames and mentally transpose them into mirror frames. Then in each mirror, "see" what quality in you was evoked by the person whose name lies behind the reflection. Look at yourself in relation to the person. What about yourself caused you to respond as you did to this individual?

As you move from mirror to mirror, make notes on your observations about yourself. You may gain surprising insights. If thoughts from these observations are appropriate to add to the descriptions you just wrote, slip them in. If you gained an insight that would be a subject for yet another chapter, mark it with a giant asterisk as a reminder for future writing.

Proofread your revised rough draft, and write a final version on acid-free paper.

> *The sad account of fore-bemoaned moan,*
> *Which I new pay as if not paid before,*
> *But if the while I think on thee, dear friend,*
> *All losses are restored and sorrows end.*

—WILLIAM SHAKESPEARE
English playwright and poet

CHAPTER 8

Adolescent Angst

How did I get here? Somebody pushed me.
Somebody must have set me off in this direction and
clusters of other hands must have touched themselves to the controls
at various times, for I would not have picked this way for the world.

—JOSEPH HELLER
American novelist

ADOLESCENCE IS a time of daring hopes, bolts of joy, undeserved despair, self-doubt, arrogant egoism, rudeness, and painful sensitivity. It's frequently a time when faith in the teachings of our parents ruptures, and we flounder among peers. We experiment, take risks, weep in secret, defile our bodies, and pray.

Remembering your adolescence is likely to be both amusing and painful. You may find that unbearable embarrassments have now become bearable and insurmountable problems have been surmounted, but don't be surprised if some memories still cause you to cringe. Think back on the times of elation as well as on the awkward occasions. Perhaps your adolescent soul was in a phase of molting. Regard it gently now.

Write a quick, careless draft to one of the following prompts, or tell about a happening you remember vividly. To rev up your writing, begin with one or more of the following prompts:

- The most fun I had in high school was…
- I felt humiliated when…
- My big goal was to…
- Mother (Dad, other) was probably right, but I still wish…
- Mother (Dad, other) was wrong, and I wish…
- A time when I disappointed myself…
- I felt different because…
- I was scared when…

David M. Seligson has devoted most of his adult life to the welfare of children. Even when he worked as a public relations director for the Portland Trail Blazers, he was creating programs for young people. In this portion of his memoirs, he remembers his adolescence.

> *I look at my father in his big easy chair made of plastic leather cracked by time, unaware I was struggling with how to reach him. I asked him often enough to get out of the glass booth that I imagine surrounded him. My voice at first impenetrable and then it became silent for I only talked to myself.*
>
> *Yet I loved him. He was kind, wouldn't yell, he just damn never talked to me about anything. I often smelled his cherry pipe tobacco when he wasn't there. I would pick up the leaves and roll them between two fingers and put his pipe, unlit, in my mouth to be closer to him, and I was, but the boyhood despair I masked and became a nice quiet kid who went around to the new suburban house and ripped out plumbing like it was cotton candy. I was angry and I couldn't tell him, nor could I tell him I loved him.*

Read your rough draft aloud to yourself or a trusted friend.

When listeners in your response group ask questions about your account, write them down. We tend to feel we've taken care of the missing information when we answer orally, and we forget to amend the writing. Later, when you revise this rough draft, you'll see your notes and remember the questions. Then you can decide whether or not to insert the requested information into your final draft.

You're ready to gather ideas for your second writing. On a new page draw a large stick figure that represents who you were as an adolescent.

On your figure's round head, draw hair styled as you wore your hair in high school. Near the margin of your paper at head level, name the items you used to style your hair.

Dress your figure in the type of shirt, blouse, or sweater you used to wear.

Draw pants or a skirt resembling the shape and length of those you wore. If brand names were important, write them down. Indicate pockets and their contents. To the side, draw the sort of notebook, backpack, or other gear you toted.

Shoe your figure with the type of footwear you liked. Draw socks or stockings if they were visible.

If you wore them, add jewelry, watch, braces, body ornaments, and include electronic items or any other paraphernalia you carried with you. (See figure 5.)

Along the margins of your page list:

- Sports you played
- A musical instrument you played
- Your favorite class
- Your favorite teacher
- Your worst class and teacher
- Your best friend
- An enemy
- Someone you emulated
- After-school activities you joined
- Jobs you had
- What you did on Saturdays
- Titles of popular songs
- A book you reread
- A movie you remember
- A TV show you watched
- Issues you argued about with a parent
- Something you did that was dangerous or risky
- Ways in which you felt inadequate
- Your appraisal of your body
- Your worries

Though your stick figure is only two-dimensional, it, with your lists, has brought you in touch with your adolescent years. You'll now be able to recollect emotions you felt at that time. If you are writing with a fellow writer, take time to explain your drawing and lists to each other; your explanations will bring back still more memories.

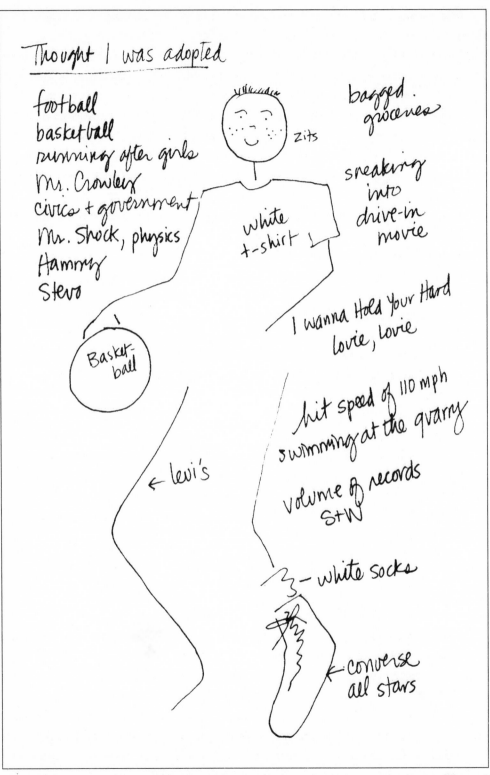

Figure 5

Write about a happening that was important to you during your adolescence. Even though the experience might not have appeared significant to the people around you, it still could have shaped your feelings about yourself or a decision you made that affected the next years of your life. To identify subjects, think back on triumphs and failures, discoveries, lessons learned, or even the giddiness or dismay following a first date.

Your account is likely to reflect your social relationships, a primary concern for most adolescents. It may show how you wanted to be seen by others. Make notes about who your friends were and why they attracted you. What about you attracted them? Which adults did you attempt to impress? What did you learn about work and about play? How did your peers and mentors help you—or lead you astray?

Your writing will be most vivid if you choose a specific incident and then imagine yourself in the location where it happened.

Use your five senses as you prepare to write your account. From a particular spot in the scene you describe, name what you see, hear, feel, smell, and taste.

Describe the people. Quote what they said and what you said. Tell what happened. Reveal your feelings at that time.

> *There came a time when the risk to remain tight in the bud*
> *was more painful than the risk it took to blossom.*
>
> —Anaïs Nin
> French writer

The next step is to experience this draft aurally. In the same way you would be kind to a stranger or polite to an alien, regard the teenage person you once were with forbearance. If your oral reading sounds like a confession, so be it. We have all been adolescents.

You know the guidelines for good listening and for responding to rough drafts. Apply them as you hear this draft.

Alan Reeder has been a singer, songwriter, teacher of children with disabilities, and university program director for teachers of students with disabilities. The following paragraph appears in a section of his memoirs about his adolescence. Notice Alan's effective integration of vocabulary from his rebellious youth.

> *The rebel in me was expressed in other ways—a long pompadour hairdo, you*
> *know the kind I mean; self-inflicted initials carved into my wrist with a razor*
> *blade; a silver chain and medallion hung welded around my neck, removable only*

if you removed my head. That was the idea. There were hands taped on a Friday night, ready to fight a perfect stranger. "Midnight auto" excursions were a source of excitement and a way to show off. Yes, the "caper" for those who know about such things.

Reflect on your rough draft by writing answers to the following questions. You may be able to expand one or more of your answers into significant additional material for your memoirs.

- How did you fit, or not fit, into your family? Into your class at school?
- What were your aspirations?
- What were your fantasies?
- What caused you to feel guilty?
- What does this show about the values of your family? About your own values?
- What was your greatest fear?
- To what extent did religious faith play a part in your adolescence?
- For whom or what did you feel empathy or compassion?
- In what ways did you help someone or play a supportive role?
- In what ways were you helped?
- What was your source of hope?

The year she was a sophomore in her Palo Alto high school, Liane Cordes was inspired by her English teacher, Ms. Johnson, to become an English teacher herself, an aspiration Liane fulfilled.

Ms. Johnson stood tall and straight behind the lectern, reading the attendance sheet in a deep, sexy voice. She didn't look like any English teacher I'd ever had.

She was dressed in a simple yet elegant gray straight skirt, matching sweater, white blouse with a red ribbon tie at the collared neck, black heels and stockings. Huge red earrings swayed as she looked up to greet each person whose name she read. She smiled the deep red lipstick smile at each one of us. When she got to my last name, she hesitated a moment, and I waited for her to massacre it. My first name was even more difficult to pronounce.

"LYE-AIN CORDS." *Even her botching my name sounded sexy. Susie Prichette giggled two rows over, and Judy Burrell smiled.*

Ms. Johnson asked if she had pronounced it right. I raised my hand. "Here," I said. "My name is Lee-ann."

Ms. Johnson smiled at me, a larger, more welcoming smile than she'd given anyone up to that point. She never lost her dignity, even amidst the snickering.

"Let me make a note of that. That is an unusual spelling. Did I get your last name OK?"

My gosh, I thought, this lady cares who I am.

"No, ma'am," I replied. "Cordes. It's Liane Cordes. You know, like tortoise. My softball team's called Cordes's Tortoises, if that helps you remember."

She laughed deep and long, her dark brown eyebrow arching playfully above her right eye. "Ah, that's a perfect way to remember it. Thank you." She winked at me and went on.

From that moment on, I sat in the front row of my sophomore English class and vowed I'd be just like her, a sexy, deep-voiced English teacher who made it a point to know and value each student. I'd dress with class and color, and I'd command respect like her by standing tall and dignified no matter what happened. And I'd be passionate about English, mostly about literature and writers. I'd read passages from The Red Badge of Courage *with drama, with heart. I'd make the words sing off the page until every kid who heard Stephen Crane's words would never want to fight or go to war. They'd all want to be English teachers, gentle and compassionate and pronouncing every student's name exactly and with great care.*

Based on listeners' suggestions, your reflections, and most of all your own intuition, revise your rough draft.

Consider having your rough draft proofread if you plan to distribute it widely or if you would feel more comfortable with a corrected final draft.

> *I think somehow, we learn who we really are*
> *and then live with that decision.*
>
> —ELEANOR ROOSEVELT
> American political leader, U.S. delegate to the UN

Some people who have used the prompts in this book have enthusiastically written rough drafts without taking time to write final versions as they advanced from chapter to chapter—a good thing to do if one's purpose is to explore the interior life without creating a lasting book. To avoid this situation, resolve now to write final versions as you proceed. They don't have to be perfect. When you make mistakes, just cross them out. If your final version is somewhat sloppy, your readers will recognize that you are a busy person, not a book publisher.

PART II

Rising Action

CHAPTER 9

Events That Shaped the Course of Your Life

Life is like a game of cards.
The hand that is dealt you represents determinism;
the way you play it is free will.

—JAWAHARLAL NEHRU
India's first prime minister

WE ARE ABLE TO control some aspects of our lives, but events and circumstances often elude our control. Employment opportunities, the economy, opportunities for education, our health, even crop failures can alter our plans. The interweaving of our wills with chance, or destiny, reveals much about us. While writing this chapter of your memoirs, you'll show how events shaped your life and how you shaped events.

First, write a quick, messy, twenty-minute draft beginning with one of the following prompts:

- A time I did not feel in control was when...
- I had to make the best of it when...
- I realized my life would be different when...

This rough draft may be about feelings you have never before expressed, even to close friends. You might wait until tomorrow to read it aloud to yourself. A passage of time between the writing and the hearing will engender perspective.

When you read your story aloud, listen to it in the same way a caring friend would listen.

In your rough draft, you may have confided about a time of difficulty or major change, a soul-searching time. If so, this story could be less easy to read to listeners than past drafts have been. Form small response groups, and remember that listeners must not judge the writer's actions or feelings, or tell outsiders about what was read.

Respond to one another's rough drafts by first pointing out an admirable aspect of the writing and then asking a question for further information.

The following excerpt is from "Family Memories" by my beloved aunt, Thelma Merrick Hicks. Her parents homesteaded in the panhandle of West Texas, where she was the eldest of nine children. Her memoirs show how weather can affect the course of one's life.

The drouth of 1917 was the beginning of a disastrous period. With no rain, the sand and wind swept the pastures clean of vegetation: Grass roots stood above the ground like coarse spiderwebs, the fields lay bare, livestock walked the fences reaching for a bite of greenery. And now came the fearful news that the United States had entered World War I. It was June 5, 1917. Induction centers were opened and the young men had to sign up for the war.

In preparation for your second writing, list dates for about a dozen events or circumstances that shaped your life. You will probably think first of occasions such as marriages, moves, career beginnings, discoveries of interests, births, and new contacts. Also include events that altered your life such as changes in health, inheritance of money, failures, and wars or natural disasters.

Alongside each date, name what happened. If you don't remember the year, an estimate will suffice. Name events as they occur to you; your list need not be chronological (see figure 6).

```
              Pivotal Experiences

      Year              Event

      '53         move to Colorado
      '59         death of Norris
      '62         admission to Michigan State
      '68         job in California
      '70         marriage
      '82         Mom's death
      '73         birth of twins
      '78         divorce
      '79         religious conversion
      '83         remarriage
      '92         joining outdoor league
      '99         starting the new business
```

Figure 6

If you're writing independently, imagine telling a good friend about one of the experiences.

> If you are writing with other people, find a partner.
> Tell your partner what happened on the listed dates. Go into detail. Tell how your life was affected. Tell how you felt.
>
> Listen while your partner relates a happening in his life. Help him consider the impact of the event on subsequent experiences. Ask how your partner was emotionally affected.

Now choose an experience from your list to write about. It may be the one you related to the listener, or it may be a different subject. Sometimes talking about what we plan to write carries us on to another subject that seems to edge in, demanding, "Write about me first!" As usual, be guided by your inclination. You'll write best when you write about the topic that fuels your enthusiasm. Think of your list as a catalyst that leads to more subjects; don't be limited to the list.

The list you made is a rich source for ideas for further chapters in your memoirs, so place it in your greenhouse file for future reference.

Write a rough draft, proceeding carelessly, freely, and impulsively, knowing that rough drafts can be changed radically. Tell not only what happened but also how your life was affected and how you felt about it.

The following excerpt, set in 1932 when she was nine years old, is from the memoirs of Betty Jean Speck. She says of herself, "I write because no other medium can give such pleasure, such depth of soul, and so many lifelong friends as does creating one's diaries, journals, letters, essays, poems, or prose."

Notice that Betty's memoirs are written in the present tense, an option that sometimes helps writers convey a strong sense of surroundings and immediacy. If the drafts you've been writing seem cursory, try using the present tense.

It's clear and cold our early December morning in Wallace, Idaho. A pale sun barely visible over the eastern mountain casts no spell of warmth. The rectangular wood and metal-reinforced trailer Daddy built, now bulges and towers, laden with Mother's canned goods. It's covered with Daddy's ten-man hunting tent and strapped down with heavy rope just like he hitches loads on pack animals. This load won't budge an inch no matter how far we travel!

Mother slowly closes and locks the front door, comes down the wood steps, then the cement steps to the street. She hands Lydia Tabor our keys since Lydia will rent out our little house until this depression is over when it might then sell. They hug one another, promising to "write often." We bid farewell to our other neighbors gathered to see us off— tears sting as I give bear hugs to my best girlfriend, Jean Tabor, my pals Habut, Vernon, and Roy Carlson and to the grown-ups. Already this morning I have walked, touched, and blown kisses to the Indian Path up our mountain that spells "big adventure," to our vacant lot where Daddy sets up my play tent every summer, to our lilac tree of fragrant spring bouquets for Mother and then lazy summer shade for childhood daydreaming, then to each room in our house, including down steep wood stairs to my best spot of all—our cellar.

In 1932, I'm nine years old, have just started the fifth grade and am in love with my teacher, Miss Alma Schilling. I'm as scared as I am sad—this seems the end of my happy childhood days as I listen to worries about thousands of Dust Bowl refugees flooding California. Will our food supply last until Daddy can find a job? Will we be able to pay rent for a decent place to live? Added to that, I whimper, "Don't they really have any mountains? Does it snow just once in awhile, maybe?"

Our new 1932 Chevy sedan begins slowly to move down Queen Street. The windows reveal an interior packed almost to the roof with bedding, linens, and clothes. I am packed on top of pillows at one side of the backseat. Clutching my doll, I wonder teary-eyed what child now has my most treasured of all toys—my dear little G.E. electric range that I could not bring. As we turn the corner I wave—my friends' faces are blurred images to treasure. Daddy and Mother drew from savings for our new car for this long journey and unknown future. Daddy will do all the driving, and Mother will hold Teddy on her lap all the way to California.

Following the guidelines for good listening and responding, listen to an oral reading of your rough draft. If you also listen to the writing of a partner or fellow writers, you may feel moved by sympathetic feelings. Listen to your reading of your own draft with sympathy, and learn everything you can from all the readings you hear.

To reflect on the spiritual dimensions of your account, write responses to the following questions. Reflection on your writing will lead to discoveries you would not otherwise make.

Was the experience transformational, and if so, how? Did you discover new opportunities for yourself?

What inner qualities are reflected by your response to the experience?

What was the source of your strength, resilience, courage, enthusiasm?

Tell about any ways in which your response to the event expanded your intellect or talents.

Laura Lyford is a medical secretary by trade and an aspiring writer. In this part of her memoirs she described the beauty of her house and then told why she had to leave it.

My husband had gone insane, and nothing I had tried to do seemed to help him in any way. I had brought my babies home to this house, watched the sun rise on so many mornings, scrubbed every corner, cooked thousands of meals there—but I had to leave. Where would I go? What would I do? I had no answer, only an urgent call that said: Get out! Save yourself!

I packed up a few changes of clothes, loaded them in the car, and drove into town. I thought I'd go to a laundromat, but I ended up at the Dairy Mart, checking a phone book for motels. I never imagined I would be starting out on my own at the age of forty-five, but I did it.

Revise the content of your draft in any way you wish. Add or delete material, and change or rearrange it. Then give it a title.

Look for documents to embellish the revised account. In albums, scrapbooks, or boxes of saved items, you may be able to find:

- Certificates
- Conscription papers
- Employment contracts
- Deeds
- Newspaper accounts
- Announcements
- Letters
- Diary entries
- Other records or documents

Decide where to insert each document, and indicate space for it on your rough draft. When you write your final version, you'll leave room to place it where you want. If you don't care to include documents, that's OK too.

Handwrite, type, or key in your final draft onto acid-free paper.

This would be a good time to begin carrying a portable notebook. Find a light-weight notebook that you can carry everywhere you go—a book to stash in the car or tote in your bag or pack. Cheap spiral notebooks work well.

Copy ideas for future chapters onto the first pages, and write drafts on the following pages. As you generate ideas for each chapter, you will list many subjects from which you'll write only two drafts. If you write the other ideas in the front of your portable notebook, then wherever you are — in a waiting room, at the laundromat, on a commuter train, or anyplace else you find yourself with a few minutes of free time— you can make progress in writing your memoirs.

The real voyage of discovery consists not in seeking new lands but seeing with new eyes.

—MARCEL PROUST
French novelist, critic, and essayist

CHAPTER 10

Evolving Ideas about Religion

Doubt isn't the opposite of faith;
it is an element of faith.

—Paul Tillich
American theologian

IN HIS BOOK *God and the American Writer*, Alfred Kazan says he considers religion to be "the most intimate expression of the human heart . . . the most secret of personal confessions, where we admit to ourselves alone our fears and our losses, our sense of holy dread and our awe before the unflagging power of a universe."

Do not hesitate to write this chapter if, in your personal spirituality, you are not committed to an organized religion. Unbelief and belief interact in the same arena. You are a contemplative, introspective person who has a relationship with religion. Most people who have chosen not to practice a religion have given the matter earnest thought about their choice. You have a story to write.

Change either of one of these warm-up prompts to be applicable to your life:

- My thoughts about religion are like (different from) those of my parents in the following ways...
- My religious education (experience)...

If you decide to read your rough draft aloud to a listener, choose someone who will be sympathetic to your religious perspective, not someone who will wrestle with your ideas. Ask that person to identify the strong features of your writing, and then find out if he has any questions about what you wrote.

If you prefer not to share your experience, read your account aloud to yourself anyway. You'll hear phrases you can improve. Listen to your voice as if you were meeting yourself for the first time.

If you are writing in a fellowship of writers: This time you will have to observe the listeners' guidelines with special strictness so you don't become sidetracked into theological debates. Remember that the purpose of the response group is not to discover absolute truth but to assist the writer in expressing his or her truth. You may need to make extra effort to suspend your own opinions and judgments. Listen to learn, and keep the thoughts you heard within the response group.

A writer has just entrusted you with an intimate, important account. Be sensitive to the soul of that writer.

Read aloud your rough drafts and respond to each reader. Say what you admire about the writing. Ask for specific information.

The Reverend John Pierce grew up in the South. An awareness of surroundings that you'll see in this rumination continues throughout his recently written memoirs, *The Sign of the Osprey.* Because he now lives in the Pacific Northwest, his current images are of cold rivers, fir trees, and ospreys instead of Spanish moss and bald cypress.

> *I was raised in a family where each Sunday we went to church. I don't remember religious conversations at the dinner table, yet, like eating breakfast, church was part of the routine.*
>
> *I was an anomaly. My parents never had to make me go. There was no pressure. Strangely, I wanted to go, yet I never understood all that was going on, only that there was a "presence" there, and I would sit in the pews as though marinating in the juices of the holy. My parents did not quite understand me, for I was drawn to God from my earliest rememberings. I also knew I was different.*
>
> *My life, like most kids' lives in the subculture of the deep South, consisted of sports and outdoor activities, fishing in the lazy bayous of Louisiana of Spanish moss and bald cypress. From there I knew the mystical properties of low-lying fog skimming the surface of the waters in the early morning light. Fish, snakes, trees, and long-legged*

cranes spoke to me of the mystery of creation. Even the damp smells of forest and lakes with the sun glistening on surface sparkles of water opened my heart to that which I did not comprehend but which I would subsequently learn comprehended me. My family gave me root and appreciation for beauty and respect for liturgy. But they could not answer the intellectual struggles of a youngster. I slipped into a kind of fundamentalism, trying to put the pieces together of biblical writ, mystical experiences, and scientific bent of mind and education. I wanted the definitive in an infinite array of paradoxes.

As a university student intent on being a doctor, I could not share what laid claim on me in early life. At the age of three, or thereabouts, I was baptized. It is one of my earliest remembrances. In an Episcopal church in downtown Shreveport, Louisiana, I walked with my parents to the back of the sanctuary and mounted two wooden steps that elevated me to an appropriate height for the rector to administer the water. I do not remember the words "I baptize you in the name of the Father, and the Son, and the Holy Ghost." I only remember the picture: a small boy, water dripping from his head, wondering…wondering.

To gather ideas on the subject of religion, reminisce about the evolution of your thoughts and feelings about religion with a partner or by yourself. Your experiences may have occurred within a framework of organized religion, or they may have been independent of formal religion. Make notes as you reminisce.

- From the time when you were growing up, is there a particular prayer or verse that you still remember?
- Did certain music used in worship or at other times hold a sacred quality for you?
- Did a worship service, such as a particular holiday service, especially appeal to you?
- Were religious observances practiced in your home?
- Did a certain place seem especially spiritual to you?
- Who among the people you knew seemed to have a spiritual quality?

If, as you grew older, you experienced disillusionment, cite instances of disappointment in:

- People
- Institutions
- Teachings you had believed
- A previous faith

How did these experiences affect your faith?

God does not die on the day when we cease to believe in a personal deity, but we die on the day when our lives cease to be illumined by the steady radiance, renewed daily, of a wonder, the source of which is beyond all reason.

—DAG HAMMARSKJOLD
Secretary General of the United Nations, recipient of the Nobel Peace Prize

Was there a time when you tried to feel the presence of God but could not? What was happening in your life? What were your doubts? Explain your emotions. How has your perception of God changed during your lifetime?

Whether God exists or not remains forever a fascination. But God, believed in or not, remains only the elected Official for the colossal job of mystery. To my mind, prayer was the real question. For prayer exists, no question about that. It is the peculiarly human response to the fact of this endless mystery of bliss and brutality, impersonal might and lyric intimacy that composes our experience of life. As the human response to this mystery, prayer, not the existence of God, is the thing to be decided.

—PATRICIA HAMPL
American writer

The following excerpt is from the memoirs of The Reverend Don Purkey, whose childhood religious experience was in a Pentecostal church in Ohio. When he became a college student at Miami University, he worked during summers in a paper mill. After his marriage, he attended a Presbyterian seminary.

I was twelve or thirteen, I can't remember, but I was in the eighth grade when I had two experiences. The first was an evangelist who was predicting the end of the world. And they always projected a certain date. I remember doing a rough calculation and saying, "Damn it! I won't get through college before he comes."

The other was a traumatic one which has as much influence in causing me to go off in another direction as anything in that period of my life. It was at an evangelistic meeting.

It was incredibly hot, an August night. I can remember the funeral fans that the women held—some of them were paper with pictures of Jesus' life, and others were palm leaf-type things—these rather heavy-bosomed women in their cotton dresses, fanning themselves. And I remember Brother Rose and Sister Bryant and their testimonies.

The evangelist was seventeen to nineteen—I want to say he was seventeen, but it is hard for me to believe that he was still in his teens. He preached on hell, as most of those evangelists were wont to do. He said that if God should send a single bird to earth every million years to pick up one grain of sand, that when the bird had totally removed the whole earth, that would be your first split second of burning in hell.

I was traumatized.

It was taken as an indication that I was being saved. I was dragged to the altar and literally thrown on my knees by a surging crowd that was hovering over me with their hands all over me, and I was weeping and crying. I can remember lots of "Praise God" and "Let's pray him through to salvation." It seemed to go on forever and ever. I had been traumatized by what had been said, by the emotional pitch of the service itself, by the physical things happening to me as an adolescent. All of that produced a kind of hysteria that was misunderstood by those who were present.

I came home that night. Inside me I said, "God, if that is the way you are, I'll burn in hell." I cried probably into the morning, finally being so exhausted and falling asleep but having decided sometime during that period that if God was like the God being described, I wanted nothing to do with God. It was an overt kind of decision. I said nothing to anyone but refused from that moment on to go back to church.

You're now used to writing quickly, without hesitation, knowing that you can later expand what you've written, remove portions, rephrase sentences, and rearrange sections. With this in mind, write about a stage in your religious evolution.

If you're writing with others, your time together will limit your development of this subject, but you will succeed in initiating this chapter of your writing.

Hearing what people in your group have written will be not only interesting but suggestive of issues you may want to address. Respond to others' drafts as you always do: find something positive to say about the writing and ask a question.

No passion in the world is equal to the passion to alter someone else's draft.

—H. G. WELLS
English science fiction writer

The following paragraphs are part of the memoirs of Aimée Ross-Kilroy, who earned her Ph.D. in Renaissance literature. Aimée now teaches, mothers her daughter Emma, and enjoys gardening.

I started attending mass again during my senior year of college. Loyola Marymount University had a chapel on campus, and every Advent they followed evening mass with a big tree-lighting ceremony in the quad. So the first Sunday of Advent seemed a good time to start attending church again, after several years away.

It was quite a shock. Apparently some changes had taken place during my absence. I was used to shaking hands with the people around me during the sign of peace. But now I was not only expected to hold hands with people during the Our Father, but I was supposed to watch as "liturgical dancers" wafted down the aisles waving lilac scarves while the offering basket made its rounds. The lights were dimmed and then brightened to heighten the feeling of spectacle as the mass proceeded. I felt a profound sense of displacement.

But in the quiet spaces of the mass I also felt a sense of homecoming. I had tried to "be Buddhist" for a while, but contrary to the beliefs of countless college students like myself, that's a tough thing to do with a paperback book and no community in which to ground yourself. I had felt that the mass had become empty and sterile of meaning, and I was looking for some kind of practice that would connect me daily and deeply to some kind of divinity. So I had stopped attending mass and started reading books.

Now, however, I felt a sense of place and safety. The chapel stretched above me and before me. The light reflected off of the white walls, the wooden stations of the cross. The scent of incense and burning candles was familiar. Like my family, the religion I'd grown up in is weird, dysfunctional even, and often unsatisfactory. But I speak its language and know its terrain. As I held my tiny white taper with its construction paper circle meant to protect my hand from the wax, I marched with all the other students through the cold clear night. Singing in front of the tree in the center of campus, I took a groping baby step toward something I still find difficult to express in words.

CHAPTER 11

Struggles and Satisfactions

*I went to the woods because I wished to live deliberately, to front only
the essential facts of life, and see if I could not learn what it had to teach, and not,
when I came to die, discover that I had not lived. I did not wish to live what was
not life, living is so dear; nor did I wish to practice resignation, unless it was
quite necessary. I wanted to live deep and suck out all the marrow of life,
to live so sturdily and Spartan-like as to put to rout all that was not life, to cut
a broad swath and shave close, to drive life into a corner, and reduce it to its
lowest terms, and, if it proved to be mean, why then to get the whole and genuine
meanness of it, and publish its meanness to the world; or if it were sublime,
to know it by experience, and be able to give a true account of it in my next excursion.*

—HENRY DAVID THOREAU
American writer, teacher, orator, gardener, pencil maker, and surveyor

THE EFFORTS WE make when we undertake any endeavor reflect our sympathies
and enthusiasms. Whether we succeed or fail, our initiative is an essential component
of ourselves. In particular, our strivings to surmount obstacles reveals our strengths, our
beliefs and values, our capability, and our courage. This chapter will guide you in writing
about times when you made a determined effort.

You'll also write about satisfactions you've enjoyed. You'll first bring to mind the
activities you find satisfying and then show how you savor at least one of them. Contentment is as much a part of our essential being as is effort.

Today, as you prepare to write, turn back to chapter 2 to review the steps of the writing process. In most of the upcoming chapters, the steps of the writing process will not be explicitly stated, but you'll follow them as a matter of course.

To assemble ideas for your writing, name the activities that have given you pleasure as a young person and as an adult. These activities might range from playing ball to sewing, from painting to swimming, from constructing a house or repairing the car to caring for a child. Name things you've done with a partner or group of people, as well as by yourself.

Write "Enjoyable Activities" as the heading for your list (see figure 7). Identify activities that have involved:

- Making something
- Using your intellect
- Using equipment
- Using your body

Also identify:

- Activities you do by yourself
- Activities you do with a partner
- Activities you do at home (away from home)
- Activities you do in a group

Write a quick description of yourself doing something that gives you pleasure. Satisfying experiences are sometimes sensory; if yours is, think of how you can include your five senses in this description. Show your satisfaction through your actions and, possibly, through dialogue.

Suggested prompts:

- When I was young, I loved to…
- An activity that has given me pleasure…
- Whenever I have time to do what I enjoy, I…
- An experience that makes me feel good is…

The following selection is by Lilly Burgard, who has loved telling stories since she was a child. She now finds the writing of stories yet more magical and says her memoirs, telling the story of her choice to be a single mother, will create a link between her childhood and that of her young son.

Enjoyable Activities

making things
- making wine
- herb box
- photo album

using head
- programming computer
- class at City college
- reading
- crossword puzzles

daytime
- lunch at cafe
- stopping at museum
- walking through park

evening
- movies
- reading
- visiting with friends

equipment
- camera
- computer
- kitchen appliances

body
- jogging
- tennis
- yoga

by myself
- reading
- walks
- sauna

partner
- eating
- concerts + movies
- sex

Figure 7

I have always enjoyed cooking, watching others cook, helping others cook, cooking for others, as well as prepping the food and not cooking it. Like the time I worked in a tremendously busy delicatessen in Ann Arbor, I never tired of cooking. It is a love.

When I was in college, I would cook a special meal every Friday night, with no guests invited. Yet, every Friday someone would drop by unexpected and I would offer a warm, luscious feast. Soon I found the apartment full of unexpected guests every Friday night. Years later I met my match. Dave amazed me. Even before he moved into our communal household he spoke of cooking in a way that resonated in my heart. The first day he arrived he made a pile of fresh pasta and had it draped over chairs and laundry stands throughout the house while he cooked huge batches of pasta sauce to can.

I had never before met anyone with this kind of attitude toward food. We spoke the same language of texture, color, and smell; the fine art of peeling garlic and drooling came easily. He loved to joke and to laugh but he was always serious about food, even in his gaiety.

"Pancakes are my specialty," I said. He said that his were better. So we had a pancake bake-off. One Sunday I served. I made a huge batch, but only Dave partook of the event. It was true, they were unbelievably good. They almost made him cry. "What is the secret ingredient?" he asked after guessing everything but the mystery item. "I have to know!"

"Pecan meal!" I exclaimed triumphantly.

The next Sunday was his turn to serve. He invited lots of guests for the event. The kitchen was completely taken over by him two hours prior to the gathering. The excitement and energy in the house thrilled and warmed me. It is a feeling I have come to associate with Home, with a capital H.

The guests arrived and all were fit in a most comfortable manner around the table that should only fit four. The food was amazing and the warmth encircled us all with a gentle hum. Dave won, hands down. I have yet to be able to accomplish this art of Home that he illustrated to me so wonderfully.

Lilly's memoirs go on to describe her wanderings in India and southeast Asia, her search for a philosophy and for enlightenment. In contrast to her travel writings, this particular entry shows her desire to create a strong sense of home.

If you're writing independently, read your draft aloud to an imaginary friend.

Something New: Guess Who the Author Is

If you're writing with a group of writers, redistribute your rough drafts so listeners won't know who wrote them. Read aloud the draft handed to you, and ask the group to guess who wrote it. Not only is this guessing game great fun but it will help you become more aware of individual writing styles, points of view, and assumptions. You'll see what about your own writing is identifiable to other writers.

To assemble ideas for a second composition, think of the advantages you've enjoyed and obstacles you've faced. Then on a sheet of paper, form two columns, giving one column the heading "Advantages" and the other the heading "Obstacles."

The following categories may help you think of personal advantages and disadvantages to list in the columns: physical, mental, educational, economic, familial, circumstantial, historical, accidental, and spiritual. Some of your listings might appear in both columns.

Now choose an adversity or hardship about which to write. It may be something you've overcome or something impossible to surmount. By writing about an adversity, you'll reveal hopes, aspirations, strivings, concerns, and emotions that are unlikely to emerge if you were to write about the advantages you've enjoyed.

At a later time, after you've written about an obstacle, write about an advantage.

Write your rough draft impulsively and rapidly so that unplanned words can emerge. Subconscious understandings and wisdom that appear can astound us. Later, when you revise the rough draft, you may decide whether to retain or discard any unexpected thoughts.

Describe not only what happened but also how you felt about the experience. What emotions did you feel? Were you guided by them or did you squelch them? Readers won't know you unless you show your feelings. A workshop participant who had worked for the Red Cross in stricken places throughout the world wrote about events that had happened and the noble work she had done, but she forgot to share her feelings and thoughts. As a result, her chapters read like dry reports. A technique that eventually enabled her to bring her emotions into her writing was to imagine herself on location and to write in the present tense, describing what she could see, hear, feel, smell, and taste. She added information about her emotions and quotations that expressed her thoughts. By using these techniques, she succeeded in showing not only what she had experienced but also the caring, courageous person she was.

> *I think that in order to write really well and convincingly, one must be somewhat poisoned by emotion, dislike, displeasure, resentment, fault-finding, imagination, passionate remonstrance, a sense of injustice—they all make fine fuel.*
>
> —EDNA FERBER
> American novelist and playwright

Read your rough draft to a loving listener, or read it aloud to yourself.

The following excerpt by Bruce Novak was written when he was a doctoral student at the University of Chicago, where he helped prepare high school English teachers. It will be published by Palgrave Macmillan in a forthcoming collection entitled *Reverence in Teaching*.

When I entered the sixth grade, I thought I was pretty much the perfect student.... What did it mean to be "the perfect student"? My grades, of course, were quite high in every "important" subject. (I had a deathly fear of, and hence developed almost no abilities in, the two "unimportant" subjects of art and physical education, but no one thought it worth the bother to offer me any significant help in overcoming my fears, because these subjects were seen to be so peripheral.) From a very young age, I learned to live for my grades, to identify myself with the grades I earned, to see the set of numbers that arrived every nine weeks on a small, pale blue card as a revelation of my true worth, in numerical terms.

My first prominent memory from sixth grade is from the performance of a skit a group of us had been asked to write. Our assignment was to dramatically portray as many of the fascinating aspects as we could of the Canadian province of Newfoundland. I remember nothing of the skit now, and very little about Newfoundland. What I do remember is that we made a bridge between the two parts of Newfoundland by staging a boat trip between the populous island territory of Newfoundland proper and the territory of Labrador on the mainland. To liven this up, and to furnish our audience with firsthand experience of the plenteous aquatic population that provided the main livelihood of our province, we had our boat crash and sink, forcing us to swim to shore amid a huge school of codfish.

I thrashed wildly on the tile floor, letting loose a feeling of primitive physical joy that as a determined nonathlete I had never had the opportunity to feel before. Perhaps it won't be easy for you to see this, but that physical feeling represented a huge emotional release for me. For the previous five years, I had acted as if I did not have a body, as if all that I was was a mind. In real life, I refused to go swimming, except under the duress of the requirements of summer camp. The feeling of my arms, legs, and stomach thrashing against the cold tiles, which I pretended were codfish, was thus a dramatic moment of liberation for me. I was portraying the desperation of a man trying to save his life by swimming through icy, choppy, fishy waters. What I felt inside, though, was the sudden sense of a life—of personal, incarnated flesh rather than disembodied, depersonalized mind—that was worth saving, a life that suddenly mattered.

Notice that as Bruce reached the part of this narrative where he broke the restraints of his earlier identity, he chose the strong nouns *joy, release, duress, liberation, desperation,* and the vivid verb *thrash.*

At your leisure, consider the spiritual dimensions of your rough drafts. Take notes as you name:

- The people who inspired or encouraged you
- The capabilities you have shown
- Instances of your creativity or courage
- An example of your resolution
- Talents you have
- Other strengths you possess
- The source of your patience
- The source of your energy

You will observe that most of the questions for reflection expose your good qualities and lead you to seek their source, bringing to light parts of yourself you may not have fully appreciated. Most introspective people are already well aware of their shortcomings and do not benefit from further reflection on them. Granted that at certain times, such as during psychoanalysis, we do need to pursue the causes of our discomfort; however, the goal of such analysis usually differs from your purposes at this time. Though you will write about disappointments in your life and in yourself, the insights emerging from your reflections will direct your voyage toward the light in yourself rather than into darkness.

Integrate your notes into your drafts and then read them aloud again. When you're satisfied that they say what you want to say and sound the way you want them to sound, think about asking someone to proofread for you.

Try asking your listeners or your proofreader to suggest titles for your drafts. The titles they propose are likely to reflect what they see as the theme of your writing, interpretations that can be surprising and may even increase your self-understanding. Remember, though, that as the author you have the right to override suggestions of every sort.

As you write your final drafts, don't hesitate to make major changes. Final versions are sometimes quite different from first drafts and often much better.

Save your writing ideas—the notes you made about activities you enjoy and your list of hardships—in your greenhouse file. Now or at a later date, write additional chapters about your struggles and satisfactions.

A Culminating Prompt

You've been writing to warm-up prompts. To go further, take time now to write to the following expansive prompt:

- I like (don't like) to think about...

This prompt can lead you in interesting directions. Play with its various possibilities and see where it takes you.

Success is never final; failure is never fatal;
it is courage that counts.

—WINSTON CHURCHILL
English politician and historian

You're rapidly accumulating chapters about critical aspects of your life. You've worked through a third of the chapters in this book, so at this time enjoy rereading all the narratives you've written so far. You may begin to notice themes, and you may also be surprised by insights.

If you are writing in a fellowship of writers, this would be a good time to schedule a special session at which everyone reads one chapter to the group at large. Bring any chapter you feel inclined to share, but if you prefer to just listen, feel free to say "I pass" when your turn comes around.

Before the reading begins, remind all participants to suspend judgment about the life or thoughts of the writer, listen to expand their own understanding, and guard the reader's confidentiality.

Share refreshments and celebrate your achievement.

You know, memoir is not court stenography. Memoir is not a video on You Tube. Memoir has a narrative. A good memoir is a person's experience, their memory, and how that experience mattered to them, emotionally, and psychologically. A memoir then, unlike an autobiography, isn't always about the truth, but perception: It is one person's unique view of the world.

—AUGUSTEN BURROUGHS
American writer

CHAPTER 12

Focusing on Your Subject

Writing teaches us our mysteries.

—Marie de l'Incarnation
Founder of the Ursuline Religious Order in Canada

OFTEN WE GIVE scanty labels to the snapshots we slip into albums. Years later, descendants will look at the photographs and wonder about the lives of the people pictured. If only someone who knew the subjects had written about them! What were the dreams and fears behind the smiling faces? What mischief did these people concoct? What is known about the horse on the other side of the fence? What happened in the shack at the water's edge? A story lies behind every photograph.

The second and possibly lengthier draft you'll write will be about a snapshot. But first, warm up to writing. Remain indifferent to mechanical correctness, and allow your writing to capture whatever memories arise. Find your fluency by writing quickly and impulsively from one of the following prompts.

- A happy period in my life was when…
- I felt self-confident and hopeful when…
- A time in my life I like to remember is…

When you finish writing, sit back and look over the story you related. Do you now see that happy period of your life in a greater context? How has that period affected your life? Consider adding information to this rough draft to provide an overview.

The account you just wrote may be so pleasant to hear that you'll want to reminisce by reading it to a friend.

Pour lemonade and sit on a porch together as you hear each other's drafts. If the weather is wintry, sip hot cider indoors as you savor the happy memories.

Now you're ready to move on to your second draft. This time you'll write about a snapshot picturing something, someone, or a place that has been significant in your life. You may have been any age when the picture was taken. The more important the subject is to you, the stronger your writing will be.

It might show:

- People you've known
- You at a certain time
- A meaningful place
- A poignant experience
- An object
- Something else that is important to you

Telling someone about the snapshot is an excellent and natural way to prepare to write. In the telling, you'll automatically find the right words and begin to arrange your thoughts; so before you start to write, show your snapshot to a friend or writing partner. Talk first about the photo, then discuss the following topics:

- Everything shown in the picture
- Things *not* shown in the picture
    - ~ The time and place
    - ~ The relationships between the subject and other people
    - ~ The story behind the picture
    - ~ Related stories this picture suggests
- Your feelings about the subject in the picture
    - ~ The way you felt when the picture was taken
    - ~ Reasons why you saved this photograph
    - ~ Reasons why you selected it today

When you write your rough draft, it's possible that your rendering will spread far beyond the scene of your photo to a greater story. Let your writing take you where it will.

Glance through your written draft to see if you indicated your feelings toward the subject. Your feelings may be indirectly indicated or stated directly.

Consider how your narrative fits into the whole of your life.

Read this draft aloud to yourself, a writing partner, or a small group of writing companions.

If family members read what you wrote, sooner or later someone is sure to say, "You've got it wrong. It wasn't like that at all. I'll tell you how it really was." Then that person will proceed to tell how she remembers it.

Who's to say which of you is correct? Maybe neither of you, or maybe both of you. Actually, the facts don't matter. What matters is the way *you* remember it. After all, these are your memoirs. If you don't recall certain facts, that in itself is interesting. Memoirs are by their nature subjective, not objective. As some insightful person said, "Don't let the facts get in the way of the truth."

> *After* Five Boyhoods *came out, my mother set me straight. "Grandma wasn't really like that," she said, defending the mother-in-law who had made her own life far from easy. "She was unhappy and really quite shy, and she very much wanted to be liked." Maybe so; the truth is somewhere between my mother's version and mine. But she was like that to me—and that's the only truth that the writer of a memoir can work with.*
>
> —WILLIAM ZINSSER
> Contemporary writer and an authority on writing

If you invite a family member to listen and respond to your rough draft, be prepared to stand by your story as you remember it. Revise and complete your writing before allowing it to be seen by any relatives or other people who may react with antagonism; their objections could dishearten and dissuade you. Jane Tompkins, author of *A Life in School: What the Teacher Learned*, mailed the manuscript of her memoirs to her editor before sending a copy to her mother. This sequence proved to be prudent because when Jane's mother received her copy, she responded with an attack that lasted over two hours. Eventually most relatives do become reconciled and gain understanding of the writer.

Suppose you don't agree with the suggestions made by listeners or proofreaders. Simply thank them for their advice, and then proceed to write the final version in your own way. Trust your own knowledge and judgment.

Because you prepared to write by first telling about your snapshot, you may not feel much need to revise your rough draft; however, if you wish, you can add information, change how you said something, cross out any part you want to omit, and rearrange paragraphs or sentences.

Consider your rough draft in light of the following questions. Take notes in response to them, as the act of writing will further your thinking.

- What does your selection of photographs show about the things you value?
- If this chapter alludes to a time of harmony or wholeness, tell about it.
- With whom did you empathize? Why?

If you would like to have your rough draft proofread before writing the final version, ask someone to check punctuation, paragraphing, spelling, and word choice.

Include a photograph of yourself in this chapter. Decide whether to lay out your text leaving room for the photograph at the top, under the title, or between paragraphs within the chapter. Write a caption under the picture, even though you gave identifying information in the body of your text. Photography shops sell acid-free, non-PVC photo-mounting products: double-stick tape strips, photo tabs, and adhesive protective photo holders. These products are suitable to use with acid-free paper.

We think of memoirs as being about the writer's own life, but occasionally memoirs are dictated by the subject to a writer who composes and edits the dictation. *The Autobiography of Malcolm X* was dictated by Malcolm X but written by Alex Haley. A similar extension of authorship occurs when a writer who is related to the subject enters imaginatively into the identity of that person to recount his story, using the pronoun I. Thea Halo wrote as if she were her own mother in *Not Even My Name* to tell the stories of escape from Turkey she had heard her mother tell.

Lisa Arkin, a dancer and dance educator, has undertaken to write her grandmother's memoirs, something she can do, thanks to the extraordinary spiritual intimacy the two of them shared and because of Lisa's detailed knowledge of her grandmother's life. When Lisa uses the pronoun *I*, she is in the role of her grandmother.

The Francesca

Yaneh and I had waited in Warsaw many, many months for the permission to leave Poland. I don't remember the details of the bureaucratic process. I only remember the endless waiting. Who in the government decides which desperate Jew gets a visa? How many bribes does it take to get the steamer ticket to leave Europe? How do the lucky ones get from Warsaw to a seaport? These questions tumbled over and over in my mind until I could think of nothing else. We pushed on every door, begged every official, sat in every waiting room until the benches and the lines and the faces behind the counters blurred together.

Somehow, we made it happen. We left our homeland behind us.

The Francesca—this was the name of the steamer on the tickets I clutched inside the pocket of my coat during the long train ride to Italy. An Italian boat, the Francesca sounded to us like a bronze-skinned, dark-eyed Mediterranean maiden, a young strong woman who would take us into her arms and carry us to a better life.

The grandmother of Lisa Arkin, Gertrude Boshnack Reitkop, at about age sixteen in Warsaw or Russia, in 1917 or 1918.

When we climbed aboard the Francesca as she was docked in the harbor, the smell of cow manure, a pungent residue of her most recent passengers, assaulted us. By the time all of the new passengers had been taken aboard, we realized that we would fare much the same as our predecessors. It was so crowded, and we all jammed together on the deck of this freighter to avoid going below to the cattle hold. There you would be overcome by thick air redolent with hay and dung. Later, as the days passed on the Francesca, we would almost get used to it. The Italian crew had no patience for bewildered passengers who tugged at their sleeves with incomprehensible questions spoken in strange European languages.

Yaneh took ill almost immediately and spent the entire voyage lying unresponsive in a dark corner of the hold. He visibly weakened day by day.

Yaneh clung to life during the three weeks we sailed across the ocean in the Francesca. When the passengers began calling out, "America! America!" he begged me to help him crawl to the deck to see this long-awaited sight. The joy and exhilaration we felt upon seeing the Statue of Liberty erased all our previous sorrows and fears. The Francesca docked just beyond her, near Ellis Island. Dozens of sallow yet hopeful faces peered over the railing, and somehow we all found the strength to clutch our suitcases and bundles. Our voices were light with laughter as people talked about the relatives who would be waiting to welcome them to America. The end of the long journey and the beginning of a new life was within our grasp.

But although the lady of liberty had beckoned, America's doors were closed to us. The Francesca's cargo of Eastern Europeans, many of us Jewish, was not allowed under America's new immigration quotas. Our type of people was being counted, checked, and bound to strict limitations. They've already reached their quota of Jews this year, we were told.

When the boat began to pull away from the dock a wailing rose amongst us. Arms stretched over the railings and hands reached out to the majestic lady who had promised,

"Give me your tired, your poor, your hungry…" Some men helped me bring Yaneh below. His eyes were glassy. None of us spoke. As the New York skyline grew smaller and smaller, the despair that settled over us crushed our spirits. The Francesca *met the open sea again.*

If you wrote about a person with whom you are still in contact, consider sending a copy of this chapter to him. He will be surprised and, if your memories are positive, pleased.

If you wrote about a place or thing, think about whether the people who were there with you or who knew you at the time the snapshot was taken would enjoy reading your account. It's likely that individuals who were personally involved will take an interest in it.

Be forewarned, however, that recipients of your chapter are likely to find discrepancies between your memories and theirs, and be assured that your memories are as valid as those of anyone else. Know that someone is likely to challenge even a trivial detail. Be prepared to smile to yourself, and keep writing.

CHAPTER 13

Transitions

The art of progress is to preserve order amid change
and to preserve change amid order.

—Alfred North Whitehead
English mathematician and philosopher

BEFORE YOU GATHER ideas for your next chapter, warm up with some rapid writing. The warm-up writing will prime your mind in the same way an athlete's warm-up prepares her body for an event. Write as much as you can in about twenty minutes, using one of the following prompts or make up one of your own.

- A time when I felt optimistic and hopeful was when…
- A time when doors were opening for me…
- I looked forward to…

If you would enjoy sharing this draft with others, read it to your supper companions this evening, or read it over the telephone to a friend or relative. Explain that you've undertaken a major writing project and that this reminiscence is part of it.

> If you're writing with colleagues, do not break into small groups this time, but sit back and savor everyone's story. Of course, you'll remember to withhold judgments, listen to broaden your understanding, and keep the readers' revelations within the group.
>
> Point out the best aspect of each person's writing, and ask about something not completely evident.

Sometimes the warm-up writing develops into a piece more major than the second composition. Always allow your writing to be as lengthy or short as feels appropriate.

If you're writing independently, go ahead now to expand your rough draft, revise it, proofread it, give it a title, and write your final version. If you're writing with a partner or circle of writers, set this draft aside to complete later, when you're alone.

This excerpt is from the memoirs of Dr. Tim Brinton. Though he ends this section when he became a janitor, he eventually went to medical school and became an anesthesiologist.

My feelings on leaving home were not regret or longing, but rather a quiet determination to prove that I could be independent, that I could support myself, and that I could "get an education." I had been away from home before for periods of up to a month, always with friends. Leaving home was an easy adjustment. I was busy with my new life as a college student. I hardly looked back toward home in Baker, forty miles away. After about six weeks I returned home for a weekend visit and to pick up additional possessions. Dad said, "You've changed."

He acknowledged the independence that I was proving to myself. With an exchange of glances, a pause, and without more words, Dad and I both understood what was not spoken. My home ties were separated. I had passed into an adult stage of my life. Dad was uncomfortable speaking about feelings and personal matters, but he was sensitive to people.

Mother asked about my laundry, my winter jacket, did I have enough bedding. She had ready cookies and home-canned fruit for my return to La Grande.

My brother Jim had just preceded me as a student at Eastern Oregon College. I joined with some of his student friends who were "baching it" in an apartment. We learned the realities of cooking and washing dishes and cleaning. Our odds and ends of dishes and utensils were barely enough to fry eggs and heat canned beans or stew. Our convenience foods consisted of home-canned fruit or jam. One roommate from a farm home occasionally received meat or chicken, which we shared. Our menu was limited by our inexperience in planning and cooking.

After a few weeks I started a part-time job as a janitor in the Green Parrot Grill.

There is nothing permanent except change.

—Heraclitus
Early Greek philosopher

Sometimes we initiate changes in our lives, but frequently they are imposed on us by external circumstances. Transitions can be beneficial or harmful. They can be seen as curses or blessings, and sometimes in retrospect we alter our evaluation of them.

To prepare to write about a transition in your life, first list changes you've experienced. Write them down as they occur to you, and move freely back and forth between the following categories, leaving at least six lines under each heading:

* Geographic changes
* Economic changes
* Changes in family structure
* Career changes
* Changes in relationships and friends
* Changes in health or physical condition
* Changes in interests
* Changes in affiliations and memberships
* Changes in beliefs or values.

From the changes you listed, circle the two that seem most dramatic or to have had the greatest impact on you—or about which you feel inclined to write. Then place your list of changes in your greenhouse file.

Find a partner. If you're writing independently, invite a friend to join you for coffee to hear about two of the changes you've experienced. If you're more comfortable confiding in the cat, then talk to your cat about transitions. Explaining the changes aloud before you write will boost your written fluency.

Choose one of the two stories you just related. When you told them, you probably found that one seemed more significant than the other or would develop as a chapter better than the other. Or, you might have found that you feel more inclined to write about one subject than the other.

Scrawl a quick, sloppy draft and then follow the now familiar process for listening to it and receiving responses.

This memory of a child's move to college is from a mother's perspective. The writer, Wanda Henson, is a nurse, teacher, and volunteer supporter of her local art museum and county government. She considers herself fortunate to have the freedom to pursue her many interests.

We took our oldest son, Larry, up to McMinnville to help him get settled in his dorm at Linfield College. It brought back memories of when I first arrived at my own dorm and how excited I was. Leaving Larry up there was not as emotionally draining as it might have been, because my memories helped me feel excited for him beginning this new adventure.

Monday I came home from school and started dinner. As usual, my final act of dinner preparation was setting the table. To my surprise, I couldn't set the table in the dining room that evening, because Larry wasn't in there playing the piano. The first thing he always did when he arrived home from school was go to the piano. I could tell how he was feeling and what kind of day he'd had by the songs he played, or the way he played them. To my surprise, I started crying and couldn't set the table. We ate in the kitchen for almost two weeks before I could bring myself to go in the dining room and set just four places at the table.

Until that Monday evening, the awareness that our family had changed forever hadn't hit me. We were still a family, but it would now be different.

Reflect on the account you wrote. To make your reflection as insightful as possible, write notes in response to the following questions:

- How were you changed by the transition?
- What resources helped you make the change?
- Where did you find your courage (resilience, energy, patience)?
- How was the change beneficial? Detrimental?
- Was destiny involved? Do you believe in destiny?

When you revise your rough draft, use arrows to indicate any rearrangement of paragraphs you'd like to make. If you plan to insert additional paragraphs, place numbered asterisks where you will insert correspondingly numbered paragraphs. Change words or phrases, and strike out sentences or paragraphs you don't like.

After you've proofread your revised draft and given it a title, find documents and photographs from the time you described. Clippings, saved letters, and scrapbook souvenirs all add interest and life to written accounts. Records of any sort give a sense of authenticity and add the flavor of the time. Photography shops and even copy shops can often improve the clarity of old photographs, so consider using them even if your photographs are not now in good condition.

Thirty-Three

Knowing others is wisdom;
Knowing the self is enlightenment.
Mastering others requires force;
Mastering the self needs strength.

He who knows he has enough is rich.
Perseverance is a sign of will power.
He who stays where he is endures.
To die but not to perish is to be eternally present.

—Lao Tsu
Chinese philosopher

CHAPTER 14

Joinings and Separations

Every parent should be charged with recounting and
sharing personal memories about their children's first hours.
Not just the commonplace details we're asked to fill in on the lined-off spaces
of commercially produced baby books, but sentiments and particulars....

—PETER R. STILLMAN
American writer, editor, and teacher

IN THIS SESSION you'll write about the arrival of a new person in your life or the loss of someone. You might write about a birth, a death, a first encounter, or a parting. Often we lose people for reasons other than death; nevertheless, those individuals leave our lives as certainly as if they had died.

Focus on the actual moments of first coming together or on the event of separating. You might have been any age when the experience occurred. Many of us retain pictures in our minds: a newcomer appearing at the door; the back of a man as he walks away; a child peering from behind a window, waving; the irregular breathing and last breath of a dying person.

Gain writing momentum with a quick warm-up. Choose one of the two following prompts or think of an alternative:

- The first time I saw...
- The last time I saw...

As alternatives to writing about the first time or last time you saw a certain person, you could write about a place or an object. Still another alternative is to use a sense other than vision. You might write, "The last time I heard…" or "The first time I felt…" As soon as you decide on your prompt, write impulsively and rapidly.

Dana Furgerson, who wrote the following segment, is a teacher, writer, and wood-carver. Her son, now in his forties, is a potter.

The birth of my son triggered emotions of such profound intensity that I remember them with exquisite clarity. Dear God, the first instant I saw my baby boy I knew what mother love was. Its fierce intensity charged through me. I felt as if the nurse who placed my baby in my arms had also handed me a sword to wield against the world.

I knew the importance of the life in my arms far exceeded mine. I would die for my baby. I would kill, if need be. I knew I could never alter this love or diminish it. I cried for joy, but a terror of the magnitude of my feelings invaded me. I was a strong woman, a struggling survivor of a pervasive, damaging mother. I knew the decisions I made at this moment would shape both my son's life and my own. I pledged to guide my son toward independence from me. I pledged to honor his being as separate from mine. But most of all, I promised my son that I wouldn't repeat what had been done to me.

The fear of becoming my mother smothered me, and an iciness enveloped my chest. I held my boy to me and chanted, "I love you, son. I love you." I would not be like my mother. I knew this now. I swung my imaginary sword and vanquished all that threatened my boy and me. I chuckled with joy. My boy, my boy.

Read your rough draft aloud to a friend who is present at this time or to a friend no longer present whom you remember.

If you are with a community of writers, read to those friends. After you acknowledge each cowriter's primary talent, ask a question formulated to help the writer add supportive information.

You're ready to gather subjects for your next chapter.

Throughout our lives we acquire new associates, friends, antagonists, and family members; and we lose people too. Separations from them may fill us with either grief or relief. Prepare now to write about people who entered into or departed from your life by listing:

- Births with which you've been closely associated.
- Close friends or relatives who have died. Give their names if you were with them or near them at the time of their deaths.
- Animals whose deaths or disappearances affected you. The slaughter of a farm animal can be a painful memory.
- If you remember the occasions when you first encountered people who became significant in your life, list those individuals.
- If you remember times of separation from people who were important to you, list those individuals. Perhaps you lost a friend when your family moved, or when a relationship ruptured, or when their personality or yours changed. Mental illness or impairment and addictions can sever close companions, and the separation of divorce often leaves vivid final memories. Take time to list people you lost due to other causes as well.

Many of the incidents behind the names you listed are subjects for important chapters. Choose any one of them to write about now. If you feel inclined to write about an experience that looks trivial in comparison with others, go ahead and do so. Your responses to the death of a pet, or some other, lesser-seeming experience, may reveal a significant dimension in yourself.

When you've chosen a subject for today's chapter, file your list of topics in your greenhouse folder for future writing.

From her home in Eugene, Oregon, Sharon Franklin prepares textbooks for publication. She wrote these thoughts about her dog, Evie, and about herself:

> *I miss Evie terribly. I miss the way she leaned into my body and let me stroke her bony little back. I miss the way she would throw her head back and look at me. I miss the way she put her paw on my foot as if to say, "I belong to you!" or snapped her lips and teeth together in anticipation of a treat.*

Evie showed me the best part of myself. She reminded me that I am not too busy to help someone I love. She showed me that sacrifice means nothing. It's just what you do. Evie also was, I think, symbolic of some abandoned part of myself. I learned to love that part.

Though Sharon was writing about her dog, she has shown us even more about herself.

Prepare to write by talking with a friend or relative about the incident you've chosen. If you kept a diary at the time of the incident, read those entries.

This narrative could begin or end with a detailed scene. To create that scene, see the techniques suggested in chapter 4. Since your chapter will probably involve telling why your subject was important to you, you are likely to relate a story that precedes and follows the detailed scene you show.

Find a partner, and tell each other about the subjects you are considering.

After you've explored your subject conversationally, write a quick first draft.

The following excerpt is taken from the memoirs of Sara Schwake, whose writing also appears in chapter 6. This portion is from a chapter about her mother's last days.

The last E.R. sojourn, where there was "little to be done but keep her comfortable," made me know it was completely right to place her gently in our car for her last ride. I got in the backseat and put my arms around her shoulders as Alan drove. She was conscious but unable to verbalize. Still, I wanted to show her something of the beauty in the scruffy, mostly barren eastern Oregon landscape. I told her to look at the rims of mountain ranges surrounding us with pale pink light in the late afternoon dusk. They were miles away, but she slowly turned to look. It's okay, Mom...we're going for a drive...together we've enjoyed this so many times before.

Hear the effect of your rough draft by reading it to a kind, appreciative listener or to your circle of writers. Ask listeners to respond according to the now familiar guidelines.

In the following excerpt, Leila McMillan Shaw describes the death of her mother, a forerunner of the first women to take leading roles in the Presbyterian Church. Her memoirs include many photographs from her family's album. The clerk at a local copy shop helped her make good duplications by adjusting the exposure and contrast. Copies of Leila's book have been placed in national and local Presbyterian libraries.

> *In early March, Mother was very ill with congestion of the lungs. My sister, Juanita, let me know that I should come as soon as possible. I completed school reports due and flew to Arkansas.*
>
> *Mother got out of bed to greet me when I came into her room. Her illness had caused her to lose the extra weight she had gained in her latter years.*
>
> *Spontaneously I exclaimed, "Mother, you're so beautiful!"*
>
> *She, with matching spontaneity, replied, "Oh, pooh," dismissing the compliment.*
>
> *Juanita helped Mother put on her robe and slippers and we sat on the porch to visit and enjoy the warm spring day.*
>
> *The next morning I sat by Mother's bed as she alternately dozed and waked. She asked whether the hyacinths were in bloom. I went to the garden and found a pink one in full flower. When I brought the hyacinth to Mother, she said, "And they will bloom again next year."*
>
> *Those were her last words to me.*

Though you "hear" Leila's mother speak only one phrase and the exclamation, "Oh, pooh," notice how much dimension her voice adds to our sense of her.

Revise your rough draft as much or as little as is appropriate for your purposes. People writing solely for themselves often find personal satisfaction in the improvements that result from revision.

Implementing the following suggestions may help you achieve a gratifying revised draft:

- Aural perceptions. If in reading your draft aloud you heard anything you want to change, take care of that first.
- Listeners' responses. If the questions from your listeners have made you aware of ways you can strengthen the writing, take care of that too.
- Showing through actions. Actions can reflect feelings—a gentle gesture or a harsh act indicates emotion. During a previous session you described a snapshot; this time visualize your experience as if it were a movie, and add movement.

- Dialogue. The use of dialogue is a very good way to show feelings. Try to find places where you can insert approximations of the words spoken. Interweave descriptions of the action with dialogue.
- Sensory description. In addition to describing how things looked, see if there are places in your draft where you can interject sounds, textures, smells, and even tastes.
- Metaphysical or philosophical meaning. You may or may not want to interpret your narrative overtly. Your description is already likely to show the energies within the experience. It might even suggest a sense of transcendence.

The revised narrative may now be given a title and embellished with diary or journal accounts, photographs, newspaper announcements, certificates, farewell letters, or trinkets associated with the entry or exit of your subject.

The following lament was written by a seven- or eight-year-old child who experienced separation when a favorite tree was felled. It's from the diary of Opal Whiteley, a precocious girl who grew up in the early 1900s in logging settlements near Cottage Grove, Oregon. Opal used colored crayons to print her diary on odd sheets of paper given to her by a neighbor. Editors corrected spelling and added punctuation at a later date.

Some Day I will write about
the great tree that I love.
Today I did watch
and I did hear its moans
as the saw went through it.
There was a queer feel in my throat
and I couldn't stand up.
All the woods seemed still
except the pain-sound of the saw.
It seemed like a little voice
was calling from the cliffs.
And then it was many voices.
They were all little voices calling
as one silver voice came together.
The saw—it didn't stop—
it went on sawing.

Then I did have thinks
the silver voice was calling
to the soul of the big tree.
The saw did stop.
There was a stillness.
There was a queer sad sound.
The big tree did quiver
It did sway.
It crashed to earth.
Oh, Michael Raphael!

Opal: The Journal of an Understanding Heart
Adapted by Jane Boulton

CHAPTER 15

Chance and Choice

*The future is a place that is created—created first in the mind and will,
created next in activity. The paths are not to be found but made,
and the activity making them changes both the maker and the destination.*

—Dr. John H. Schaar
Professor and author, University of California, Santa Cruz

WE WORK HARD to achieve our goals and we construct our lives as best we can, but we also succumb to events beyond our control. Throughout our lives we interact with chance. Like partners dancing, we lead part of the time, but our partner, Chance, swings and turns us and changes our steps. Wisdom lies in knowing how much to lead, how much to follow, and how to find beatitude wherever the dance takes us.

You're about to write about the interplay of choice and chance and acceptance of outcomes, but first, warm up to writing.

Paying no attention to mechanical correctness, write impulsively and freely from the following prompt:

- I had to make a difficult decision when…

We've all had to make difficult decisions, but if your decision was too agonizing to write about today, file this prompt to use when you are ready. It's a powerful prompt that will lead deep into the story of your soul.

If you are not ready to travel inward this far, write instead to the following prompt.

• A choice I'm glad (sorry) I made…

Alone, with a partner, or in a small group, read aloud about the difficult decision you made. Today, in similar circumstances, you might make a different decision. Remind your listener or listeners to be sensitive to your frailties and to remember that you told them about an especially trying time in your life.

As we listen to each other's stories, it is best to assume that we have all made mistakes and to remember that our decisions were based on past circumstances and understandings. Suggest that your listeners respond by commenting on the strengths in your writing and asking a question designed to elicit more information.

Prepare for further writing. On a fresh sheet of paper, write two lists in columns, one down the left side of the paper, the other down the right side. Entitle one list "Fortunate Experiences" and the other "Unfortunate Experiences." Then name your experiences in the two columns in whatever order they occur to you (see figure 8).

After compiling your lists, you might notice something curious: the same experience appearing on both lists. If an event that at first seemed disastrous later brought certain benefits, then it is both disastrous and beneficial. An opportunity lost may have motivated us to find a satisfying alternative. Adversity or suffering may have taught us certain important skills. Some writers have felt new appreciation for their lives after surviving a serious illness or disability. A fortunate outcome does not invalidate the unfortunate aspect.

In the same way, fortunate experiences sometimes sour. A promotion, a marriage, a discovery, even a windfall can all have unexpected dark sides. Decide whether to place such events on one or both lists.

> *Life is a series of collisions with the future;*
> *it is not a sum of what we have been but what we yearn to be.*
>
> —JOSÉ ORTEGA Y GASSET
> Spanish philosopher and essayist

Consider telling a friend about one of your more influential experiences. Perhaps you can bring it up casually while dining together or talking on the telephone. Initiate the conversation by mentioning that you've been remembering a time when…

If you are writing with fellow writers, find a partner. Tell your partner about any one of the fortunate experiences and any one of the unfortunate experiences.

Listen while your partner does the same thing.

Fortunate Experiences	Unfortunate Experiences
piano lessons	house fire
Jessica's friendship	losing piano
Mom's new job	Mom not at home
big recital	Dad's girlfriend
date to prom	Shawn's ulcer
scholarship	debts
meeting Ashley	allergies
pregnancy	pregnancy
my sales job	dropping out of school
promotion	Mom + Dad's divorce
taking in Shawn	taking in Shawn
Ashley's patience	Shawn's arrest
move to Nebraska	low-wage job
promotion	car broke down
Shawn's job	debts
big garden	Ashley's depression
new job	no health insurance
bought piano	no vacation time
Ashley's improvement	Dad's stroke
bought insurance	
trip to New Mexico	
joined writers' group	

Figure 8

Write your rough draft.

The ways in which we cope with adversity are frequently more revealing than the ways in which we respond to happy circumstances, so consider writing about a time that tested you. Furthermore, although we don't often enjoy writing about our failures, doing so shows a great deal about ourselves and, rather than alienating readers, tends to draw them closer to us. Expressing our weaknesses and flaws usually humanizes us to our readers.

To make your writing vivid, recall the most emotional moments of the experience. Visualize yourself in a particular place at a certain time; describe what you saw, heard, smelled, felt, thought, and did. Be as specific as possible. If you can remember what someone is likely to have said, or what you said, add quotations.

Read your rough draft aloud, listening to it as if it were written by someone else you love.

Doug Finn, author of the following account, described himself as "a musician, a writer, a husband, and father who has lived for fifty-six years and is still trying to figure out what it's all about."

The motor puttered and the wind washed over my face, whipping my clothes against my body. It was a little 180cc Yamaha that I had bought about six months ago—about five months before Barb told me I should leave, that she didn't want to live with me anymore. I cried then. It was the only time she or our daughter, Heather, had ever seen me cry. Heather was only four. I doubt that she remembers that now.

I loved the wind against me. I loved the feeling of being enclosed by nothing, the sky for a ceiling, the ground for a floor. I was on a little dirt road that ran up into the mountains west of Tucson. I had already left the desert behind and now the trees were oaks and pines. The dust rolled up behind me and filtered into my nose, bringing a dry, musty smell. It was hot. I wore jeans, a T-shirt, and a small, white helmet.

I could take the road pretty fast, thirty-five or forty, except where the curves were sharp. The road wound around, climbing steadily, and it was full of rocks. The vibration numbed my hands and made my forearms tingle.

Divorce was imminent and devastating. We had been married five years. We had shared life, made a baby, taken care of each other, each in our own way. I didn't know what she wanted, but she had become the center of my love, and thinking about life without her was looking over a cliff into black, cold, empty space.

The sun was shining, the green oak leaves shuddered in a slight breeze. On my left the mountain rose almost straight up, and on my right it dropped almost straight down, and there was no reason to live. I was alone. I hadn't seen another human for over two hours, since leaving the outskirts of Tucson. I would be alone now, and I couldn't live that way. There was nothing to live for. And all of this, the trees, the sun, the sky, the wind, wasn't enough. I needed to share it.

I knew how easy it would be. Just don't lean, don't turn. Get the speed up to forty or fifty, and at the next left turn go straight.

I had no brilliant illumination. God didn't speak to me. I didn't come to realize that my life was worth living after all. I just didn't do it. I carried my despair back down the mountain, back to the city, back to my job and all the mundaneness of my life, and in some ways that despair is still with me today.

But I made a decision. I exercised my free will. I went on. And the part of the stream of life that my life has touched since that time has been different because of me.

The draft you've just written may lend itself to deeper examination than have previous drafts. If you'd like to ponder it, respond to the following suggestions. Some may not work with your draft, but others will. Write about:

- What you learned from the experience
- Qualities found, such as resolution, compassion, sacrifice, service
- What, in retrospect, you observe about yourself
- Instances of:
    ~ Creativity
    ~ Intuition
    ~ Inspiration
    ~ The animating force, the source of your strength
    ~ Any instance of mercy
    ~ Grace
    ~ Compassion
- Ways the experience affected your doubts and beliefs
- The significance this experience has had in your life
- Whether at any time during the experience you had a sense of transformation

If you want to cut pages of your rough draft apart to make room to insert additional paragraphs, do so.

> *Get rid of the tendency*
> *to judge yourself*
> *above, below, or*
> *equal to others.*

> —ABHIRUPA-NANDA
> Buddhist nun, sixth century BCE

Now is the time to think of a title for your narrative. Titles may best be written last because we don't know exactly what we'll say or what its impact will be until after we've completed the writing.

Consider enhancing your final version by adding letters, photographs, or other documents. If you have kept a journal, insert entries from it directly into this selection. Journal entries written at the time of a past experience will inject a strong sense of immediacy and also show the person you were at that time.

The following excerpt is from the recently completed memoirs of Joanne Randolph. She had ten copies made for members of her family; but now additional relatives and friends are requesting copies of her book for themselves, so she's returning to the copy shop to make more.

For days after the surgery, reports would dribble in, saying this or that test was negative, no problem. And then we'd wait for the next results of other tests. My tension would build up and then explode in tears, and my dear husband would simply hold me until I was all cried out. Then I'd feel strangely peaceful and able to go on.

My massage therapist was wonderful, but not able to break through my fear and tension; I couldn't sleep without drugs, couldn't breathe naturally. I was full of tension, so she sent me to an acupuncturist she knew.

In one session he improved my breathing, and in the second my sleeping. But it was his great Jewish wisdom that healed me as much as his acupuncture. He told me I was strong and I denied it, and he said, "You're here, you're strong." He said I had just lost my confidence in myself and needed to let go and just jump. "There's good stuff on the other side of this, but you have to punch your way through." He said more, but this is what impressed my memory so deeply.

My fight back to normalcy—and beyond—started that day. Shortly after, I joined a twelve-step program, Adult Children of Alcoholics, and for five years gently prodded myself to look back on painful times and heal them. It's a long process, but it helped me let go of some faulty conclusions I had made about myself. From ACOA I went on to Co-Dependents Anonymous and started to learn why I was a "people pleaser" even when I was hurting myself in the process.

My husband says I'm easier to live with now, though my changes have caused some changes in him. He says he couldn't figure where I was coming from before, and now he can, at least sometimes. Everything has a price, I guess. My life is so positive and enjoyable now, any price isn't too high.

About five years after my surgery, a question popped into my head: If I could have my breast back by giving up the wisdom and peace I had acquired, would I want to go back? I didn't know the answer. When another year had passed, I knew: I would never want to go back.

If you have not yet completed the warm-up writing, look back at that rough draft. Reflect on the difficult decision you had to make:

- Can you discern how the experience affected your life? If so, add thoughts about this.
- Was there any time during the experience when you had a sense of transcendence or of being in touch with something larger than yourself?
- In what ways did external events and your self-determination interact?

Follow the same process of revising, proofreading, and writing a final version that you used when you wrote about the fortunate or unfortunate experience.

Toward the end of his life, my father, twice a widower, married again.
Shortly after the wedding, my new stepmother, whom he had known for only a few months, began to show signs of dementia. My father had macular degeneration, and caring for a spouse with dementia was extremely difficult. I was concerned about him, and I gently asked if he felt he had to take care of someone he had not known long.
His answer was reproachful but instructive: "How many ways can a blind 87-year-old be useful in this world? Of course I will take care of her!"
—James E. Sabin
Professor of Psychiatry
Harvard Medical School

CHAPTER 16

Aspirations

When I am … completely myself, entirely alone …
or during the night when I cannot sleep—
it is on such occasion that my ideas flow best, and most abundantly.
Whence and how they come I know not nor can I force them.

—WOLFGANG AMADEUS MOZART
Austrian musician and composer

WE HAVE ALL SET goals and dreamed dreams, and we've succeeded in realizing some of them. From the time we were young children, we've had notions about what we wanted to be when we grew up and the kind of people we wanted to become. Our ideas have shifted many times as we realized what was possible and as our interests and inclinations changed; and as long as we are healthy and vital, we will continue to aspire toward new purposes.

Though we find satisfaction in our accomplishments, many of our good intentions, dreams, and strivings never become manifest. They may not even be apparent, and yet they are the greater part of our efforts. Like the underwater bulk of an iceberg, most of our aspirations are out of sight. Only our closest confidants and we ourselves know what we would like to have achieved.

As you write this chapter, you'll make visible an important part of yourself as you confide your intentions and dreams.

Today, you'll first capture ideas. On a full sheet of paper, draw the outline of a large cloud. Inside the cloud name the goals you've had from childhood up to the present time, including your current aspirations. You may randomly place the words you write in the cloud.

Name your dreams in the following categories:

- Vocation
- Profession
- Athletics
- Arts
- Society and culture
- Ecology
- Home life
- Self-improvement

If you had a difficult childhood, you may not have had an opportunity to dream and formulate aspirations when you were young. Some children are so overwhelmed with simply surviving that their intentions must focus on the immediate situation. If your childhood was like that, then your cloud may not be as full as the cloud of someone who had a comfortable, well-nurtured childhood. You are to be commended for any aspirations you managed to generate.

Write about your aspirations, starting with one of the following prompts or by beginning in your own way:

- One of my aspirations has been to…
- I wanted to be (become, be like)…
- A goal I've had…

Read your rough draft aloud to yourself, a friend, or a small group of writers.

Marlene Elam Neal never did become a champion swimmer, but she is now a member of a theater troupe in Oakridge, Oregon, called Zero Clearance. Here is an excerpt from her chapter "Swimming."

> *I was about nine years old when Red Cross swimming lessons were coming to town in that summer. There had been many articles in* My Weekly Reader *at school that I was faithfully practicing so I would be prepared for the river. I dived for marbles in the bathroom sink, retrieving them with my teeth. I took my baths all in total immersion with my eyes wide open. I flutter kicked and Australian crawled with my*

belly touching nothing but the piano bench. I saw every Esther Williams movie avail-able in my small town. Mother fastened my braids on top of my head; I was ready.

Ferne M. Kellow, a teacher and avid genealogist, enriches her charts with stories about family members who might otherwise be known by no more than their names. Though Ferne was discouraged from pursuing a teaching career, she went on to earn a Ph.D. and has taught at all levels, from kindergarten through graduate school. She says the obstacles in her own life have made her a good tutor of students who contend with difficulties.

I went to Southern Oregon State College on a full scholarship—determined to become a teacher—never dreaming that my teeth might prevent me from fulfilling that dream. Dr. Smith was my freshman speech teacher and broke the bad news to me the day I gave my first speech. After class she spoke to me in the hall, saying, "The college will never certify you as an elementary teacher with a lisp as bad as yours." Lisp? No one had ever told me before that I had a speech impediment. To say that I was shocked is putting it mildly. The only suggestion Dr. Smith had was special speech classes.

For three years I took remedial speech training for no credit. At the end of my junior year that teacher told me, "Your lisp is impossible to correct. You're doing every-thing right, but the gaps between your teeth just let the air through. I'm sorry. We can't approve you for student teaching." The silent screaming in my head started again.

But I've always been stubborn and don't take being told I can't do something lightly. So, I set out to find a dentist who could put in an extra tooth and fill in the offending gap. The first dentist I found said that he would do it for around one thou-sand dollars, an outrageous price for a starving college student. The second dentist told me seductively, as he ran his hand up and down my leg, "I think I can help you." Naive as I was at the time, I realized that his price was even higher than the first. Finally, I discovered Dr. Thompson, a Medford orthodontist, who was horrified that the college was trying to keep me from teaching because of a problem that he thought was minor. He agreed to put braces on my teeth to correct the problem. Adults, it seemed, could have their teeth straightened. The college finally agreed that if I was willing to go through all that I could become a teacher.

No other technique for the conduct of life attaches the individual so firmly to reality as laying emphasis on work: for his work at least gives him a secure place in a portion of reality, in the human community.

—DR. SIGMUND FREUD
Austrian physician and psychologist

You first captured your dreams in a cloud. Now you'll draw a trail on which you'll trace work you've done, making a path of memories from which to choose a subject. On a new page, draw a wide, meandering path, and within its borders name the kinds of work you have done from childhood until now (see figure 9). Include:

- Chores
- Schoolwork
- Work in the home
- Training for a job
- Vocational and professional work
- Work for causes
- Volunteer work

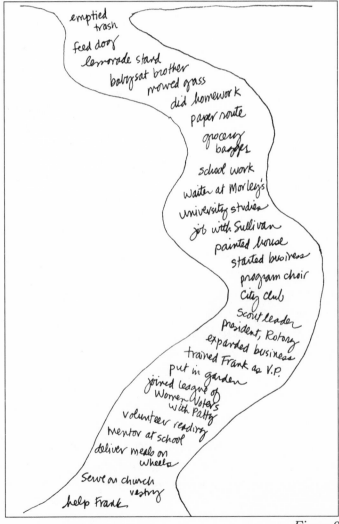

Figure 9

Now build three pillars of words that show the people, causes, and goals for which you have willingly donated work, time, and money. At the top of three columns write the headings "People," "Personal Goals," and "Causes."

Under each of these headings, list the people on whom you have spent your effort or money, the goals you have invested in, and the causes you have supported. You may have deferred or even sacrificed your own needs or pleasures in order to further greater goals.

Scan the scope of your efforts and achievements. Look at the pathway of work you have done, and then read the lists of people and goals you furthered. While reviewing these lists, make notes about the specific jobs you did and efforts you made that led to feelings of satisfaction, harmony, and proportion.

Now you are ready to write about your work and the causes you've worked for that were satisfying or frustrating. Describe your aspirations, your attempts, rewards and outcomes, and your feelings. You needn't focus only on worldly success; a humble service can be as gratifying as a renowned achievement.

Not all our efforts are successful, but when they do make a difference in the life of an individual, and especially when our actions contribute toward improved conditions for many people, then we have the satisfaction of sharing in the work of great leaders and statesmen.

Debra Burgess-Mohr has written about her efforts to promote racial justice. The demonstration described here took place in 1967, when Jim Clark, a sheriff who had turned fire hoses and dogs on demonstrators in Selma, Alabama, came to Oregon. Debra says, "There was a certain rage that helped me feel purposeful and determined."

High summer clouds drifted overhead on the day of our march in Eugene. I walked with Henry, Frank, and Lila as we led some fifty people: students, clergy, faculty members, a few housewives and businessmen down Thirteenth Street on campus. We'd made our placards—CORE Congress of Racial Equality. CORE Rally Student Union 10:00 A.M. Sat.

And we sang, "We shall overcome…we shall overcome…"against the thrumming sputter of police-mounted motorcycles.

On campus we were greeted with scattered whistles and cheers. Moving on toward town, the response was mixed: puzzlement, disgust, surprise, anger, and a few friendly smiles. Down on Broadway, in the heart of downtown, I saw people

I knew: a couple of lawyers, an architect. The children's pediatrician watched us for a moment, waved, then went on with his business. Two women, mothers of Amy's kindergarten classmates, saw me and called out, "Hi, Debbie." I had no clue about how they viewed this issue, but my God, I wished they cared.

We moved on to the plaza and stood in front of a fountain where a sculpture of bronze fish leaped and flashed in the water and sun. Henry gave a rousing speech about how black Americans were denied decent housing, jobs, and good education. He ended by outlining our plans for CORE's fund-raising events over the coming year, all in support of the Civil Rights workers in the deep South. Frank and two other U of O students spoke about the importance of student involvement.

Then, just as we were regrouping to start back to campus, I heard the shouts: "Nigger lovers!" A small group, maybe a dozen men and women holding a crudely lettered banner reading, "White Citizens for Christ and White Brotherhood," stood around two pickups. An egg hit Henry on his arm. He ignored it. I was impressed by his cool, unbending dignity.

"Dirty Commies!" one man yelled, and spit at us. "Go to Russia. We don't need your kind around here!" Frank glanced at the man as if he were air; then he and Henry, Wally, and Roy Brown closed ranks to take the lead and we started back up the street.

"Niggers! Go back to Africa where you belong." An egg smacked me on the back of my head. It hurt and felt warm and runny as it trickled down my scalp. Luv's hands tightened on mine, Henry's voice rose, and we all sang, "We shall overcome… We shall overcome… some day… some day."

While alone or among other writers, read your rough draft aloud. Listeners should know to suspend judgment, listen with an open mind, and honor the confidence of the writer.

Ask listeners to point out the strengths in your writing and also to ask a question.

> *It is when you are really living in the present—working, thinking, lost, absorbed in something you care about very much—that you are living spiritually.*
> —BRENDA UELAND
> American writer, editor, teacher of writing

To reflect on your writing, use the following suggestion:

If you prayed for help in achieving your goal, write down what you probably said in your prayer.

Reread your rough draft, looking for instances of:

- Courage
- Devotion
- Capability
- Service
- Energy
- Intelligence
- Intuition
- Grace
- Times when you allowed your self-interest to be superseded by regard for others

Revise both drafts you wrote for this chapter, have them proofread, give them titles, and write final versions.

> *Doing good to others is not a duty. It is a joy,*
> *for it increases your own health and happiness.*

—Zoroaster
Persian prophet

Chuck Selden has been a fish biologist, a lawyer, and a bookstore owner. He has a passion for ice hockey and has played the game into his seventies. In this part of his memoirs, he remembers taking part in a military operation when he was a young soldier.

It was Christmas in Korea. The year—1951. I was a jeep driver in a medium artillery battalion. Our quarters were six miles back from the front. We had forward observers on the front line. Their job was to be on the lookout for enemy targets that could be shelled with 155mm projectiles. Those observers were not going without a full-cooked Christmas dinner if our mess sergeant could help it.

The hot food was placed in thermal murmite cans, each about the size of a lard can. We must have had five or six murmite cans. The nobility of this mission was so great that our captain, the head of intelligence, had volunteered.

We started the trek to the front in two jeeps. Things went well until we reached the last quarter mile or so. The grade alone would not stop us, but the underlying ice was to give us fits. Not even chains helped. We proceeded on foot with cans strapped on our backs, slipping, sliding, and cursing but bent upon our goal of reaching the bunker where our observers were sure to be eagerly awaiting our arrival.

Come to think of it, no one had called ahead to tell them what delight awaited if they could just hold out till we got there.

We slogged to the top. We found the bunker. We thrust back the soggy, clammy GI blanket hung for a door. There was a glow inside. We burst in with the Christmas cheer and the food.

There was total surprise. Our observers told us they had already eaten with the infantry!

Look back at the many ideas you captured for this chapter. From your cloud, your meandering path, and your lists of work for people, goals, and causes, circle subjects for future chapters. Then store these ideas in your greenhouse folder.

When people are serving, life is no longer meaningless.

—John Gardner
American political activist
Founder of Common Cause

PART III

Climaxes and
Revelations

CHAPTER 17

Confronting Crisis

Out of suffering have emerged the strongest souls;
the most massive characters are seared with scars.

—E. H. Chapin
American Unitarian minister

CALAMITOUS EVENTS test us to the marrow. Our immediate response to distress reveals both our weaknesses and our strengths. Later reflections about our reactions are likely to disclose regrets and good intentions that will never be known beyond ourselves unless we confide them in our memoirs.

This chapter will help you write about a time when you were tested, a time when you were forced to react to a crisis in your life. The way you would respond now to a similar problem might be different. We don't always look back on past actions as wise or admirable, but we learn with experience. Your response to the crisis will show the person you were then; your reflections will show the person you have become.

If, as you write to one of the following warm-up prompts, you grow warm, your breath falters, and you weep, you can be certain you have identified a critical experience about which to write. A writer's physical reactions are a reliable indicator that the subject matter is significant. Commend yourself for narrating a part of your life that may be difficult to write about but is very important to include in your memoirs.

Choose one of these prompts for this first rough draft, or create your own:

- I despaired when…
- An agonizing hour for me was when…
- I didn't know what to do next or how to go on when…

When we're young, we think these things only happen to other people;
as we get older, we realize we are those other people.

—Vladimir Nabokov
Russian-American writer

Read your rough draft aloud to yourself or to a confidant—or read it silently to yourself. As you listen to it, you're likely to hear phrases you'll want to change. You may also notice that you need to give more background so readers will have a full context in which to understand it.

Important advice for partners and groups: As you listen to the account written by someone else, you may be so caught up in that writer's experience that you will be tempted to give advice, or you may feel an urge to tell about a time when you suffered a worse plight, or you may find that what was catastrophic to the writer seems ordinary to you.

Restrain yourself from evaluating the writer's experience or recounting your own experience. Such commentary will not help the writer achieve candid, frank memoirs. Instead, respond only by recognizing a strength in the writing and asking a question.

Gather ideas for your second draft.

Crises often involve loss. Write notes for yourself about the following kinds of personal loss you have known:

- Loss of a person due to
  - ~ Death
  - ~ Divorce
  - ~ A geographic move
  - ~ A mistake
  - ~ Betrayal
  - ~ Changes in one or both of you
- Loss of an opportunity
  - ~ A relationship
  - ~ A career
  - ~ A chance for change or growth
  - ~ An opportunity missed because you turned away

- Loss of a belief
  - ~ In a person
  - ~ In a teaching
  - ~ In an institution, organization, or profession
  - ~ In a religion or philosophy
- Loss of self-control
  - ~ Toward a person
  - ~ While at work
  - ~ With drugs or food
- Loss of health
  - ~ Physical
  - ~ Mental
  - ~ Spiritual
- Loss of security or belonging
- Loss of self-confidence or hope

Certain words on your list may seem to pulse with energy. If so, even though you might feel an aversion to the subjects they name, they are likely to be the most powerful and revealing topics you can choose.

Kathryn Steadman, a Reiki practitioner of hands-on healing, writes fiction as well as devotional materials, poetry, and essays. Kathryn's memoirs tell about a loss she suffered when she was only eight years old—a loss of innocence, of childhood.

The butterman pads down the hallway to my bedroom on his soft, slippery soles. He leaves no imprint on the green shag carpet. The door to my room opens without a sound. He sits on the side of my bed and removes his brown, wing-tip shoes. Was it ten minutes ago or much longer since I knelt on my knees and recited the Our Father?

The porch light shines through the shutters over my window. I begin to count (the butterman puts his finger against my lips, shhh) the slats of light. His fingers smell like pencils.

My legs feel the cool breeze of air as the bedspread is lifted into a tent that the butterman can climb inside. I count the slats backwards.

My flannel nightie, the one that began with the red flowers but has faded to pink from so many washings, is pushed to my waist as my panties are pulled down and untangled from around my ankles. I multiply the slats of light two by two.

He pushes against me and I close my eyes to the light. I smell lemon meringue pie on the butterman's breath as he heaves and sighs. I burn as the butterman pours his yellow into me. It hurts forever. It burns a hole into my soul. A hole I build my life around.

When we write about ravaging losses, the opening words are often the most difficult to find. You don't have to start at the beginning of your story. Begin anywhere. You could first describe the scenes that replay themselves in your mind and later narrate the events that led to those scenes.

Your loss may be personal, or it may encompass your family or community. Poignant memoirs have been written by people exiled from their homes.

Though Chief Joseph was a diplomatic leader who abided by treaties and strove to maintain peace, he and his people were forced off their Oregon homeland in Wallowa Valley. At first they did not fight; but later, when pressed into war, they fought for their freedom. They lost, were captured, and were never allowed to return home.

It is cold and we have no blankets. The little children are freezing to death. I am tired. My heart is sick and sad. From where the sun now stands, I will fight no more forever.

—CHIEF JOSEPH
Heinmot Tooyalakekt
Nez Perce chief

Rejection brings another kind of crisis. You might begin a draft with these words:

- I felt rejected when…

Write rapidly, not pausing to consider what you say. Reflection and revision are best done later.

When you read this draft aloud, listen to it the way a gentle soul-mate would listen. Be a compassionate friend to yourself.

We react to crises in many different ways. Fear sometimes causes us to withdraw from others. We may react with anger and defensiveness. To reflect on what you've written, write answers to the following questions:

- How did you react, and what emotions underlay your reaction?
- Sometimes when a crisis strikes we feel betrayed—by a friend, a family member, or God. Tell about any feelings of betrayal you experienced.

- It has been said that the human condition is to betray and to be betrayed. If, in your crisis, you betrayed someone else, or yourself, explain how that was so.
- Another facet of the human condition is the longing for reconciliation. Did you find reconciliation with a person, with yourself, with God?
- Sometimes forgiveness is involved. If forgiveness is part of the story of your crisis, tell how you forgave, or were forgiven, or have been unable to forgive.
- You may have accepted your loss, or you may not have become resigned to it. How do you feel about it now?
- If you have come to see your loss as leading to gain and do not now regret it, explain how this is so.

Reread your story, looking for the following underlying qualities in yourself and in others. Write paragraphs about how you find these qualities manifested or absent:

- Faith
- Compassion
- Generosity
- Hope
- Resolve

The memoirs of Jan Adams relate a time when her husband, Jack, was caught in an impossible career predicament. A New York agency hired him as director at the same time it implemented "key limitations in personnel and finance" and reduced his assistant's salary. The secretary resigned, leaving Jack to untangle insoluble problems.

My easily spouted philosophy that "people can be happy anywhere as long as they get into a community and make friends" was crumbling. It's not easy to "fit in" when you're struggling with overwhelming circumstances. Even the church seemed filled with successful people while our own discouragement caused us to feel awkward and out of place. I remember fondly the Russells, a caring couple who reached out to us and still remind me (through a little glass ladybug they gave to us) to "never underestimate the power of a simple kindness."

We went to parks—talking, walking, and sharing our search for solutions. I developed a dislike for ducks, which were plentiful in these locations and somehow became a symbol for me of hopelessness. (I have since grown to appreciate them on the lake where we happily settled in retirement.) None of my newly acquired counseling skills seemed to work for me. I remember telling a friend that we were trapped and had no choices. She unsympathetically replied, "You'd better find some." True, but difficult under the circumstances. I realized how "misplaced" I felt when a trip to J. C. Penney's made me homesick! Or when I took our Christmas letter to a copy shop to have the employee look at it and ask, "You're from Oregon? And you left? Why?" That echoed my sentiment as my dream of a grand new adventure dissolved into a nightmare.

In October I withdrew from the Blanton-Peale Institute and moved into a job-searching mode, not my favorite activity. After discouraging possibilities (long hours, low pay,) I received a call from Phyllis Jean Rodgers, Jack's cousin who was a high school counselor in New Jersey and who had heard of an opening in Edison. I protested that I couldn't do that because I'd never worked with high school students. P. J.'s unsympathetic response: "You've got transferable skills. Go for it!" So that was the risk that Jack's desperation pushed me to take, leading to a happy discovery and a wonderful career opportunity for me in future years.

Jack was able to quit his job and gradually recover from the trauma of that pressure.

CHAPTER 18

Longings

Prayer is not asking. It is a longing of the soul.

—MAHATMA GANDHI
Spiritual and political leader of India

WHEN WE RESPOND to a work of art—a passage in literature, a painting, a photograph, or a strain of music—we create a tie that connects us. At one end is the work of art; at the other end is a place in our souls. The reaction to a poem or a prayer is about the person who reads it or prays it, as well as about the poem or prayer. When we explain why a particular selection is meaningful to us, our explications are partly about the object and partly about ourselves.

This chapter will guide you in writing about what it is in you that responds to a work of art or an object, as well as about the work itself.

If you are writing with a partner or fellowship of writers, select a work of art that moves you. Bring it to your gathering. It could be something from one of the following categories or from outside these categories.

- Prayer
- Poem
- Selection of music
- Passage in literature
- Visual art, sculpture, or something crafted
- Familial blessing

To start the flow of words and ideas, write spontaneously about a time when you felt a strong emotion. You may choose any emotion, such as grief, fear, relief, bliss, exhilaration, compassion, remorse, anger, outrage, love, pity, despair, or determination.

Begin with the following prompt:

- A time when my feelings were intense…

When you read this rough draft aloud, imagine that the best friend you ever had is beside you, listening.

This prompt could lead you into passageways of your life where you experienced extreme distress. These are the times when we fervently seek understanding and reassurance. Reading aloud about these experiences may cause the voice to quaver. To recall one's emotion can trigger tears. If you are able to share your story with two or three people, your writing will benefit from their responses; however, this time you may prefer to read what you've written to a single listener.

Sensitive Responding

What should you do if someone in your writing group cries—or if you do? First, realize that the writer has succeeded in identifying and writing about a meaningful experience. Commend the writer for having the courage to explore a significant issue. Pass the tissues, and share the emotion in an accepting, sympathetic, nonjudgmental manner. Keep in mind that you'll say nothing about the writing outside of your group, and proceed to respond as usual.

Memoirs are written in the narrative genre, but they can include your poetry, letters, journal entries, essays, and prayers.

When Lisa Rosen wrote about her longing for a child, her writing took the form of a poem. Before her death from breast cancer, Lisa lived with her husband, Don, and dog, Orion, in a charming house where the garden sprouted thimbleberries.

Sarah Speaks

For years I ran with my heart
to a place that took me close to ground
close to the cool smell of clay.

Across the river
was a dream

printed in topaz
and in that bee-gold glow
where every seed that longs for form
is granted abundant body,
one of me walks with my own young son.

And everywhere his small fingers
are touching happiness.
He's fanning them to feel
the pattering sift
of tumbling pebbles,
he's sweeping them through the air
to point at birds,
he's clasping his fig cake
and reaching for me.

Watching, but marooned
and barren,
I would practice letting go.
I had only to soften my fists
to understand surrender.
I could unfurl my fingers
balled dense as tree burls
and, little by little, let
the exhausted reach
of my heart relax.

Little by little I stopped counting moons,
stopped drizzling pomegranate seeds
into my supper cup. I bent toward
the small face that made a family
of Abraham's face and mine, and said good-bye.

With empty arms, I got up
and began walking the slow mountain
of forgiveness toward Hagar.
Ages later, when that traveler
came stroking the frayed thread

of my old prayers,
naturally I laughed
thinking of the brittle rind
my body had become.

Is anything too difficult
for the Lord? he asked sharply.
I knew it was
the sizzling voice of God.

I grew hot and small
as girlhood then
and fear gushed from me
in a lie: I didn't laugh.
Ah, he said, but you did.

If you are writing independently, take time now to reflect on the draft you've just composed. If you are with other writers, put the following suggestions aside to reflect on and write about at a later time, before you revise this rough draft.

- Ponder where in your account you reveal the quality of tenderness in yourself and the quality of patience.
- What was your source of courage?
- Where did you find hope?
- How were the hidden parts of yourself affected?

Now you are ready to write about the object you identified as meaningful to you. Your writing will flow more readily if you first tell a friend or writing partner about the art or craft you have selected. In the same way that young children naturally learn to talk before they learn to write, experienced adult writers verbalize mentally before writing. If we've been composing silently while doing chores and tasks, that preparation enables us to commence writing without hesitation when we sit down at our desks. Speaking aloud to someone is even more effective than composing silently because the presence of a listener gives awareness of how our sentences are working and where further explanation is needed.

First, read, show, play, or sing whatever you selected. Then tell:

- What was happening in your life when you were drawn to your selection
- What you interpret it as saying or expressing

- What emotions or attitudes you relate to in the selection
- What this selection reflects about yourself
- How your life has been affected by experiencing the selection

Dare to ramble as you write your rough draft. Since you have prepared to write by speaking, you already know what you intend to say and how you'll say it; but what you say unexpectedly will produce insights, so allow unplanned thoughts to emerge. They're more likely to flash from your subconscious if you write speedily, without forethought.

A prayer by Marianne Williamson has been especially meaningful to Adrienne Lannom, who created fifteen homes that she shared with her first and second husbands, four children, and six grandchildren. Adrienne is a retired researcher and editor.

Here are two lines from the poem and Adrienne's reflections:

"may we all be blessed;
may we find our way home…"
What I know intuitively as "home" has often appeared in dreams at critical times in my life. Even in its various dream guises, I have always recognized it as the place of my earliest memories of myself.

I remember my home—my "real" home—the one I reach back to and search for in corners and closets and dresser drawers.

My mother tells me we will leave it and move to a bigger home in a better place far away. I was nine. At least I feel nine in the memory, although accuracy would demand that I say I was a year beyond that. It was in the spring of 1944.

I begged her to let me stay there—in that two-family house we shared with my cousins and aunt and uncle. I remember lying on the daybed in the dining room under the picture of God. That I believed it was a picture of God would've been a surprise to Mom and Pop, if they'd known. I have no idea what happened to that picture. I don't remember seeing it in the new house or anywhere again.

I became lonely and homeless for the first of many times. I learned to be alone and to search for home. As I grew up and was on my own, I made and remade new nests and found or was given others to share them with me. But then I didn't find new friends, not like the ones I loved most, the ones who sustained me, the ones I'd lost— Evie, Lucy, Tomy, Louis, Billy, Tessie. It was a big step up from the familiar Italian-Irish neighborhood in Queens to Riverdale and the Upper West Side of New York. Only I never left Queens. It was real, it was me. It loved and nurtured and comforted me. It let me be who I was without comment or criticism. It let me fit comfortably in my own skin. It didn't push to change me, to make me grow and compete for my place. It let me live with sorrow and birth and death, without fear. It stayed hidden deep within me, so deeply I often forgot it was there, but I dreamed it alive many times.

When I need to find me, that's where I am. In the patch of lawn near the garage in the backyard—Auntie's clothesline edging the paved driveway. The sun heating the brick walls and the back stoop where my cousin and I dried our hair on Saturday afternoons—mine primly braided to tame it, Evie's rolled with rags to curl it for Sunday mass at St. Joan of Arc's. Uncle Frank in the downstairs kitchen cutting the boys' hair, and occasionally the girls', the Met broadcast or an Italian-language station playing opera recordings loud enough to discourage conversation or mute the sounds of disagreement. The five blue stars on the banner in the front window for the sons and husbands "in the war." My cousin Louise, ill and slowly dying in the big bed in her parents' room by the window that overlooked the yard and caught the morning sun, her sister Lucy angrily scolding Evie and me for forgetting her suffering and letting the back door slam as we chased through the house and up the stairs, rounding up brothers and cousins for a game of ball or king-of-the-hill in the vacant lot behind the house on a summer afternoon.

If you're writing independently, ask a trusted friend to listen, or just read your rough draft aloud to yourself in a comfortable, private setting.

Take notes as you reflect on this rough draft. Write about any ways your experience with your subject brought about:

- Transcendence
- Illumination
- Energy
- Serenity
- Reverence
- Resolution
- Compassion
- Spiritual presence

Memoirists sometimes ask how they'll know when they have revised their rough drafts enough. Occasionally a draft seems right without any revision. Sometimes we make a few changes and get a feeling of "There!" Many people revise and revise until they sense it is right. For more information on revision, see chapter 28.

The two chapters you have just completed have brought you yet closer to the center of your spiritual labyrinth.

> *One must not lose desires. They are mighty stimulants*
> *to creativeness, to love and to long life.*
>
> —Dr. Alexander Bogomolets
> Department of Pathologic Physiology, Second Moscow University

If you are writing with fellow writers, plan a celebratory gathering at which each participant will read one chapter, not to exceed a set length of time. Remind everyone to observe the guidelines for good listening and responding. Pass cake and fruit, and savor a feast of words and sweets.

CHAPTER 19

Love

*He who loves feels love descend into him
and if he has wisdom, may perceive it is from
the Poetic Genius, which is the Lord.*

—WILLIAM BLAKE
English poet and painter

LOVE IS A GREAT mystery. In all its guises—altruistic, familial, erotic, and communal—it brings joy into our lives. When our offer of love is rejected, we wince, may bleed emotionally, and sometimes we grow thick, protective scars. When love fades away, our souls become dusty dry.

We cannot concoct or contrive love. It is a gift. We can create opportunities for love to appear, and we can nurture the conditions in which love thrives, but ultimately love comes or it does not. We are blessed or not.

*I was dead and now I am alive.
I was in tears and now I am laughing.
The power of love swept over my soul
and now I am that eternal power.*

—JELALUDDIN RUMI
Turkish Sufi poet, thirteenth century

As you write this chapter you'll remember times when love kindled your being. Such times may be fleeting or enduring, but always they are tender and sweet.

Our essential first experiences of love occurred when we were very young. The love we received in infancy prepared us to form emotional bonds and enabled us to become empathic people.

Most of us sensed that we were loved, whether by a parent, grandparent, or someone else. To initiate your thoughts and words on the subject of love, write quickly and spontaneously about the person who loved you when you were a child and how that love was expressed:

- As a child I received love…

If you were not loved, then write about that circumstance.

> *Love is patient and kind; love is not jealous or boastful; it is not arrogant or rude. Love does not insist on its own way; it is not irritable or resentful; it does not rejoice at wrong but rejoices in the right. Love bears all things, believes all things, hopes all things, endures all things.*
> —I CORINTHIANS 13:4–7

Read aloud your rough draft, whether singly or with other writers.

Gather ideas before you begin your second writing on the subject of love. On a large sheet of paper, name some objects of your love as you were growing up. You may name more than one of the following—or none.

- A pet
- An adult
- A classmate or friend
- An idol
- A teenager or young adult
- Another person you have loved

The following selection is by Joan Pierson, a Presbyterian minister and a spiritual director. Earlier she taught comparative literature and English at the University of Oregon.

Twice I have been sick with love, and twice people have been sick with love for me. I speak of four people here, not two, and this arithmetic says something about the strange and bitter asymmetries of loving.

I learned early about the vicissitudes of love. When I was four I went to a little preschool at a neighbor's house. Each morning my mother would take my hand and walk with me one block uphill and then, turning to the right, half another block and across the street to Vera's, and there she would leave me with half a dozen little girls and four little boys.

One of the boys was Ralphie, and he loved me. I still had my long golden curls and the assurance that I was very lovable. Ralphie would offer up most of his snack to me. He shared with me books and toys, and more than once snatched from another child a toy I coveted and put it in my hand. I never had to ask. By some strange alchemy of love he simply understood what would please me.

In the middle of that year I became quite ill with infected ears, a common child-hood happening in those days before sulfa and penicillin. The doctor came with his black case and took from it a horrendous needle, with which he lanced my ears. I remember struggle, tears, screams even, followed by an abrupt end to pain and many comforts—attention, ice cream, new games and toys.

The illness went on for days, with unpleasant visits from the doctor and daily dosings with bitter medicine—mouth, nose, and ears. And then one day, Ralphie, who missed me, longed for me, came to visit. His father brought him, and he carried, wrapped in toilet paper, his favorite toy, a nearly new red fire engine.

How lovely, how generous. But at the very moment Marie let them in the front door, a life-changing mishap occurred. My mother, in her haste to get downstairs to greet our company, made a mistake in the medication she was giving me. Into my ears went a stopperful of nose drops—no damage done. But up my nose went the fiercely potent eardrops. My head was afire. I screamed and screamed. And Ralphie, downstairs, bolted for the door, followed by his apologetic father. He dropped the fire truck, and later my little brother loved it.

Eventually I returned to Vera's preschool. Ralphie was still there, but he avoided me all the days till summer came and his family moved to another neighborhood. And so I learned very young that love, that powerful emotion, is also fragile and can disappear forever when it is too hard-pressed.

Sometimes our love is never revealed. Quietly we pulse with the pleasure and the pain of unexpressed love. Make another list, written or mental, of the people you have loved in this way.

> ***At Last***
> *You have come*
> *and you did well to come*
> *I pined for you.*
> *And now you have put a torch to my heart*
> *a flare of love—*
> *O bless you and bless you and bless you:*
> *you are back…*
> *we were parted*

—SAPPHO
Greek lyric poet
(c. 615 BCE–c. 570 BCE)

Immerse yourself in memories as you write a rough draft about a time when your love was strong. Look for the uniqueness of your experience. Love pays little heed to prescribed rules. It may flame in our hearts for people forbidden to us by social norms. It may violate the conventions of eligible or heterosexual coupling—yet it is undeniable. You may decide whether or not to share the rough draft you're about to write with listeners. For the moment, write candidly. If you decide to withhold this selection from friends or fellow writers, feel free to say simply, "I pass."

Remember a time when you felt intense, overwhelming love. Write about how you met your beloved and about your increasing emotion. Your story may describe both spiritual and sexual feelings, feelings of longing and of unity.

Though the boy mentioned here noticed me only once and spoke a single sentence to me during a week at camp, I still remember him and the way I felt.

> *We were at church camp in the mountains, where the pine-strained wind was so dry and cold it pricked our nostrils. In a corner of the mess hall, away from the clatter of dinner dishwashing and the whoops of boys in a game of chase, Sydney played the piano. He was older than I. Tall. Chocolate-brown hair. A manly chest. An inviting grin.*

I stood with other kids gathered around the piano and watched his large hands shape the chords as we sang hymns of hope and love, "Breathe on me, breath of God. Fill me with life anew," and my chest expanded with the swelling of the songs until prickles showered down my back. Our voices braided into tones that tightened my throat with sweet longing, longing for God, longing for him. I closed my eyes and imagined kneeling beside him, drinking from the chalice his lips had touched, swallowing God's gift—and I yearned.

If you are still with the person you loved intensely, you may enjoy reading this rough draft to him or her. If you are no longer with that person, slowly read your account aloud, recalling the sensations you felt. Consider reading this remembrance to a dear friend.

Advice to listeners: Set aside conventional expectations about love, and open your hearts to new possibilities and truths. Real life often deviates from the plots of romance novels, and we do not always follow the advice of our elders. Avoid judgmental thoughts, listen to learn, comment on the strength of the writing, and ask questions that will help the writer render a full, rich account.

If you are writing with a partner or group of writers, you probably have a sense of whether your fellow writers will be sympathetic or might condemn your feelings. We become vulnerable when we confide powerful feelings. If your listeners are respectful, read this draft to them.

Pat Vallerand did not expect love to enter her life in the way it did. This part of her memoirs shows the unpredictability of love. Pat continues to be devoted to and live happily with her partner of thirty years.

Something very strange was happening here. Something completely out of my control.

I was confused. But I did know that my feelings were intense—a deep, fervent, yet reverent feeling of love and longing. Different from any love or longing I had ever experienced before. As if my soul were waking up to a gift from the divine.

Cheryl and I had met at the First Baptist Church when I was attending the university and was new to town. My background was quite different from hers. She had grown up in that church, her father was a well-respected local banker, her mother the church organist. I had grown up in the Catholic Church in Lewiston, Maine, a French Canadian with parents who were working-class immigrants. I noticed her immediately. I think what drew me to her was her sense of assurance. But not an egotistical kind of assurance. An assurance that was grounded and open.

She was intelligent and had an incredible sense of humor—an understated way of seeing the absurd in most everything. She reached out in a selfless, loving way to others that I could not help but admire. She was particularly drawn to reach out to those others tended to overlook.

We had both signed up to accompany the church's youth group, which was traveling by train to attend a national Youth for Christ Conference in Illinois. Through a strange series of events, we both ended up traveling separately from the church group, arriving in Urbana ahead of them by plane, me from California and Cheryl from Portland. Alone and somewhat anxious in this new setting, I spied Cheryl across a large auditorium of thousands of people and became her roommate for the duration of the four-day conference.

It is still hard for me to describe what happened during those four days. But in that atmosphere of love and divine power, I knew I had found a soul mate. A friend like no other.

Talk was the thread that wove the friendship together. We spoke about everything that was important to us—our lives and spiritual goals. I had never felt so comfortable talking about these intimate subjects with anyone before. No matter what I said, she seemed to accept me—a truly new experience for me. She continued to amaze me with her intelligence, humor, and caring, and I also came to see the depths of her spiritual grounding.

When we returned from the conference, we cherished and nourished this newfound friendship. I was living on campus. Cheryl, who was also attending the university, was living at home with her parents. But we didn't let that impede our progress! We made time to meet to continue our talks.

I knew my feelings for Cheryl were intense, but I did not realize how intense until one day when I was sitting in the living room of my cooperative house with a housemate, Mary, and saw Cheryl walking toward the house to join me for lunch. Mary, whose back was to the window, stopped the conversation by saying, "I guess Cheryl is here." I jumped and said, "How do you know?" Her reply came with a smirk, "It's obvious from the look on your face."

The comment stunned me, but I put it out of my mind for the time being. This was 1970, after all. I had no understanding of what it meant to fall in love with another woman. But fall in love I did.

It became clear to me that Cheryl's feelings were as strong as mine. But we didn't have any idea what to do with those feelings. For a time, we channeled them all into those endless talks. Hours of talking. We met between classes and talked. We skipped classes and talked. We called each other on the phone and talked. We met at church and talked.

All of this intercourse resulted inevitably in sharing deep and painful issues for both of us. Of course, discussing hurts and traumas led us to a strong desire to provide comfort—both emotional and, as we grew closer, physical, the physical comfort we had both been deprived of growing up in our families.

When Cheryl spoke to me about the hurts in her life, I felt them as strongly as she did. I ached and cried with her. She ached and cried with me. And finally, we held each other in a deep, passionate, loving embrace. Oh, what a feeling. What a sense of arriving—arriving home. Arriving to something sacred and complete.

Respond in writing to the following questions for reflection. Some of the answers you write are likely to develop into paragraphs that you'll integrate into your draft.

- What does the love you felt show about yourself?
- Did you intuitively know something about your beloved?
- Did you sense a vitalizing principle or sacred presence?
- What did your relationship mean in the overview of your life?

A Smile and a Gentleness

There is a smile and a gentleness
inside. When I learned the name

and address of that, I went to where
you sell perfume. I begged you not

to trouble me so with longing. Come
out and play! Flirt more naturally.

Teach me how to kiss. On the ground
a spread blanket, flame that's caught

and burning well, cumin seeds browning,
I am inside all this with my soul.

—JELALUDDIN RUMI
Turkish Sufi poet, thirteenth century

Not everyone has experienced a loving marriage or partnership. If your attempts to find a mate have been unsatisfactory, write about your expectations and your disappointments. If you found fulfillment in other ways, write about the close, supportive relationships you've had with particular friends, or colleagues, or children.

About your rich and satisfying union, list:

- The ways you complemented each other
- Pleasures shared
- What you most appreciate about your beloved
- Mutual achievements
- How you've supported each other through difficulties
- The source of resilience in your relationship
- Feelings of devotion or compassion
- What enabled you to transcend times of stress or dissatisfaction
- A time or times when you seemed to be in a world of your own

Love does not consist in gazing at each other
but in looking outward together in the same direction.

—ANTOINE DE SAINT-EXUPÉRY
French aviator and writer

To edit your draft, check to see if you've described your beloved. Facts about size, coloring, and dress are less important than the impressions you had of that person.

Quotations add life and individuality to descriptions of people. If you can remember something the person once said, or used to say, insert it.

Descriptions of typical reactions also help readers know a person. How did your beloved show anger? Worry? Happiness? What caused your beloved to feel those emotions?

If these specific suggestions seem to fit into your writing, describe habitual gestures, the sound of the voice, and the way your beloved moved.

As you describe an experience you shared, describe yourself too. Tell how you felt both physically and emotionally.

What qualities in yourself were enhanced by your relationship with your beloved? Did the love you shared give you a sense of something larger than yourselves? Was there a time when you felt your love to be sacred? Holy?

When you write your final draft, leave space for photographs of the people and animals you have loved.

And one of His signs is that He created for you spouses from your own selves
so that you find tranquillity with them, and He creates the love and mercy
between you. Therein are certainly signs for people who think about things.

—QURAN 30:21

CHAPTER 20

Flip of the Compass

As Gregor Samsa awoke one morning from uneasy dreams
he found himself transformed in his bed into a gigantic insect.
He was lying on his hard, as it were armor-plated, back and when
he lifted his head a little he could see his domelike brown belly divided into stiff
arched segments on top of which the bed quilt could hardly keep in position
and was about to slide off completely. His numerous legs, which were pitifully thin
compared to the rest of his bulk, waved helplessly before his eyes.
What has happened to me?…. It was no dream.

—FRANZ KAFKA
German novelist

LIKE GREGOR SAMSA, many of us have awakened to new and disorienting realizations. The familiar, safe life we took for granted shifted into a new landscape until
even the bedrock under our homes cracked. The points of the compass that had always
indicated security and rightness quivered off course.

Profound disruptions occur and disorient us at any age: a parent departs, someone
we love becomes alcoholic or mentally ill or abusive, a trusted spouse prefers someone
else, we are stricken with illness, someone we love dies.

The disruption, however, is not always negative. We get a lucky break. A scholarship
opens doors into a new world. We find ourselves in an unexpected career, living a different lifestyle. We discover we have aptitudes, talents, or callings we didn't know we
had. We realize we aren't the person our parents hoped we would be—or the person we
thought we were. We discover a letter that reveals a new way of understanding a relationship, see why someone did what he did, learn a secret. We see the world differently.

The Cyclone had set the house down, very gently—for a cyclone—in the midst of a country of marvelous beauty. There were lovely patches of green sward all about, with stately trees bearing rich and luscious fruits. Banks of gorgeous flowers were on every hand, and birds with rare and brilliant plumage sang and fluttered in the trees and bushes. A little way off was a small brook, rushing and sparkling along between green banks, and murmuring in a voice very grateful to a little girl who had lived so long on the dry, gray prairies.

—L. FRANK BAUM
American children's author

Soon, you're going to write about a time in your life when you were faced with unexpected circumstances and had to relinquish your earlier assumptions, but first, warm up to writing. Choose one of the following four prompts:

- In my family, we never talked about…
- We talked about… only when… was not present.
- I didn't learn about… until I was…
- When we talked about… the words we used were…

> If you're writing with other writers, tell a partner how you anticipate writing to one of these prompts.

Note: Certain subjects are sometimes taboo—among them, a reprehensible relative, financial scandal, sex, someone's past life, and some physical conditions. The banned subjects are often of major importance. If they were not considered threatening, they could be discussed casually; it's because they are loaded with implications that they must be squelched. The dynamics of our families cannot be understood without identifying the dangers indicated by the silenced subjects. As a writer reminiscing about your family, you may now speak about what was unspoken.

A milder form of censorship is restriction of vocabulary. Euphemisms are often substituted when direct speech seems harshly illuminating. Euphemisms are often selected for aesthetic reasons. Another form of restriction occurs when certain subjects are discussed but only under guarded conditions, behind closed doors, or among only particular family members. This, in itself, is interesting.

If your family talked freely about everything, then write about the liberation and lack of censorship in your family. If your family seemed always to talk about the same thing, tell about that.

Write for about fifteen minutes, then share your draft with a friend, relative, or fellow writers. Ask your friend or listeners to respond by first indicating what they like about your writing and then asking a question about something you didn't tell.

Marlene Elam Neal grew up in Westfir, a tiny picturesque town nestled under fir trees in the Cascade Mountains. As a young mother, she traveled and lived in other places, but now she again lives near her childhood community. She teaches Bible class to four-year-olds.

> *In my family we never talked about religion. It wasn't until I was almost adult that I gained a clue as to why not. My mother had been raised very strict German Lutheran while my father's family had leaned toward Christian Science. I had been baptized as a baby in the Lutheran Church, but since I grew up in a small mill town I had always gone to Sunday School at a Community Church. It started out Baptist but was Presbyterian by the time I was in my junior high years. Dad later became a Mason, so the only disparaging remarks I ever heard were against the Roman Catholic Church, which I was somehow led to believe was all wrong, and I became very proud to put down Protestant whenever called upon to fill in a blank that said Religion. It now reminds me of a friend's teenager who, when asked by some girls if he was a Christian, replied, "No. I'm a Baptist."*

Do you already know the subject of your second draft? You may readily identify a time when your assumptions and expectations about your life fundamentally shifted. If so, you know what you'll write about. Many people think of a time when a relationship with a person changed. A woman in a workshop wrote about her discovery that her older sister was really her mother. Realizations even less astonishing jar one's personal view of the world.

Your life may have taken an unexpected turn when something you could not anticipate interfered with your plans—or provided opportunities. You might have found yourself living in a new place where the rules and expectations were different. The money you relied on could have ceased. Someone you adored or emulated disillusioned you. Your employer or some other authority did something surprising. A new person assumed the role of authority. A belief you held became implausible.

The reorientation could have come from within yourself as you grew to know yourself better. A teenage writer wondered why he dreamed of boys, not girls. Talents and aptitudes may emerge. An aspiring actor realized he could succeed in a career on stage but would live far from home and lose the sense of community he shared with his rural farm family. Conversely, we often become aware that we do not have sufficient aptitude to fulfill long-held dreams. These sorts of recognitions destabilize us. The compass swings wildly. We have to reorient ourselves.

John A. Callahan, a chemical microscopist, has developed analytical instruments to control air and water emissions at industrial plants such as pulp mills. His pleasures are clog dancing and singing, and acting with a troupe that performs in public schools. This part of his memoirs tells how his life suddenly changed.

> *A difficult time was when I came home from work and my wife was not there. My younger daughter told me that she had gone to the local junior college to practice her typing…. My wife suffered from mental problems and her actions were not always predictable. She would often go for long walks with the dog, and I didn't know when to expect her home.*
>
> *When it got dark, I began to worry about her. I called my married daughter and asked if her mother was there. She said that she had been but left. My wife was gone all night. She wasn't home by the time I had to go to work the next day. When I got home that evening, it appeared as if she had been in the house during the day, but she wasn't home. I went to her typing class, hoping she would be there. She wasn't. I checked all the places and people that might know anything about her. I found out nothing. I could tell, though, that she had been in the house during the day. She was just avoiding us. My life had to go on, however. I still had four kids living at home. It wasn't easy. I was concerned for her welfare but was powerless to do anything about it.*

If you have not already discerned your subject for this writing, then name:

- A shift in relationships that surprised you
    - ~ Familial
    - ~ Among friends

- ~ With people at work
- ~ A change in physical well-being
- ~ An unexpected disability
- ~ An enabling achievement
- ~ A death
- • Times when circumstances changed your mind-set
  - ~ A new place
  - ~ An opportunity lost or gained
  - ~ Sudden hardship or affluence
  - ~ A surprising change in yourself
  - ~ Revolutionary ideas
  - ~ A new role
  - ~ A shift in values

> *I know well what I am fleeing from but not what I am in search of.*
> —Michel de Montaigne
> French essayist

Because you're writing about a major change in your life, this topic is likely to require more time to narrate than previous subjects. Throughout the coming days you can enhance your quick first draft by adding background to show your life before the change and to explain the impact of the shift on the rest of your life. At this time, write about the particular event of your realization.

An easy way to begin is with the words "I was…" If you are writing in a fellowship of writers, give yourself at least thirty minutes to initiate this draft.

After working as a paralegal/investigator for many years, Cheryl Roffe left the legal field to pursue what she says is a simpler, healthier lifestyle more congruent with her spiritual values. She is a volunteer mediator with a nonprofit community mediation agency and a photo archivist in a historical museum.

My world disintegrated in a single day—August 11, 1970. It was my only day off from the cannery, where I worked during the summer to earn money for my college tuition. I was nineteen years old, and a devout Christian whose goal in life was to find a career in which I could be of service and provide healing to a suffering world. I'd always excelled at what my family considered the important things—academics, handling duties and obligations, being an exemplary "Christian" girl. I'd always been "on track," in spite of the periodic questions and doubts that had been surfacing in my mind since I was nine or ten years old.

Well, I certainly got off track on this particular day—in fact, I derailed dramatically and decisively. The day started calmly enough; I remember sitting in the living room painting an oil paint-by-number scene of a mountain landscape and listening to music on the radio. I was alone and felt very peaceful.

Suddenly, out of nowhere (or so it seemed to me) came the thought, "Fuck God!" I was stunned and horrified. To use such a word, and in connection with God, too! It was certainly not a word I used in everyday life; nor did anyone I associate with use it. I thought I'd committed the unforgivable sin that the preachers kept warning us about—blasphemy of the Holy Spirit. I tried to erase the obscene words, but the more I tried, the worse it got—those two words repeating themselves over and over again in my brain, louder and louder and louder.

In a matter of moments, the structure on which I'd built my nineteen years of life was shattered. For I believed that if I could think such a thought I could not be what I thought I was. I could not be a Christian, I could not be a respectable person, I could not help others because I was in dire need of help myself. No one who was worth anything could have ever thought such a thought, I was sure.

All day long, the inner war continued. By the time I went to the cannery to work the night shift, I was completely lost in nightmares. The words had expanded into images—visions of violence and sex and all the taboo things I had never thought of before, or at least, had never been aware of thinking about.

I had known there was evil in the world—we heard about that constantly in church. But I had never dreamed that so much of that evil was in me, as well. I was shocked, devastated, and shamed to the core, and had absolutely no idea what was happening to me or what I could do about it. I couldn't believe that someone who read the Bible and prayed every day could be seeing and thinking what I was seeing and thinking. Certainly no one I had ever talked with, or heard speak at home or at church, had ever mentioned anything like this.

When lunchtime came, at midnight, I was desperate enough that I had to do something. I had always kept my private affairs to myself—I did not even discuss them with my family. But this was too overwhelming—I was terrified that I was going crazy, or worse. So I called home. My father answered the phone. I couldn't explain what was happening to me—I hardly knew myself—and I could not articulate the ugly, revolting things that were going through my mind. So I simply asked him to help me because "the Devil was trying to take over my mind."

Cheryl has described the day her life lost its moorings. Her dramatic depiction prepares us for further narration about a spiritual struggle during young adulthood and an eventual reorientation. Like Cheryl's draft, the one you have just written is also likely to function as an opening for a longer chapter. Your readers will want to know how you coped with your disorientation and what impact it made on your life.

Read your rough draft aloud to yourself or to listeners. If, upon hearing it, you would like to revise it to be more vivid and to convey a sense of immediacy and presence, review chapter 4.

Write reflective paragraphs in answer to the following questions:

- What were your fears?
- If you prayed, what was your prayer?
- How did you direct your anger?
- Throughout the time of reorientation, whom or what did you trust?
- What gave you your sources of self-confidence?
- Where did you find the energy to do what you needed to do?
- How did your beliefs or assumptions change?
- What resulting good, if any, came from the "flip in your compass"?
- How have you now reconciled your feelings about the experience?
- What dimensions in yourself did your reorientation reveal?

> *How true it is that what we really see day by day depends less on the objects and scenes before our eyes than on the eyes themselves and the minds and hearts that use them.*
>
> —Frederic Dan Huntington
> First Episcopal Bishop, New York

You're now ready to revise your rough draft. Add to it, change it, rearrange it—or, if it's already the way you want it to be, leave it as it is.

Read aloud your revised rough draft once more before having it proofread and writing your final draft.

It's possible that the kind of writing you have just completed would fall into a literary category called "coming of age" or "rite of passage." Such writings are usually about the loss of innocence. The main character emerges from one world into another where he may confront evil or have to accept disappointment or disillusionment. Novels reflecting this theme are often about adolescents, but rites of passage continue to occur as long as we confront destabilizing changes.

May today there be peace within.
May you trust your highest power that you are exactly where you are meant to be.
May you not forget the infinite possibilities that are born of faith.
May you use those gifts that you have received,
and pass on the love that has been given to you.
May you be content knowing you are a child of God.
Let this presence settle into your bones, and allow your soul
the freedom to sing, dance, praise, and love.
It is there for each and every one of you.

—MOTHER TERESA
Roman Catholic nun

CHAPTER 21

Inner Peace

Calm Soul of all things! make it mine
To feel, amid the city's jar,
That there abides a peace of thine,
Man did not make, and cannot mar.

—MATTHEW ARNOLD
English poet and critic

THE HUMAN CONDITION encompasses both peace and turmoil; they are inter-woven through our psyches. A complex mix of external and internal factors determines our vulnerability to distress and our ability to find peace. Many of us teeter between a place of inner calm and a tendency to fret, so we are grateful for periods of repose.

To write better about the times and the conditions in which our souls find peace, we must also acknowledge and consider the episodes when our feelings war against other people, toward the world in general, and even against ourselves. You'll first write about causes of turbulence in your life, and then about how you find peace.

This writing, by a woman who does not want members of her family to identify its author, shows how the characteristics of her husband tarnished her inner peace.

Jerry's moods are the motivating factors of his life, and during our marriage I set
about the business of trying to positivize his moods by giving him what he wanted.

His predominant mood is that of a soldier waiting for an ambush. A year in Vietnam as well as his violent upbringing gives him the sense that the world was always out to "get" him. He is ready to fight at the least provocation, and if none should appear he creates one to fill his need. Even when he tries to relax in the evenings by watching TV, his loud, voracious fingernail biting is a sign that his guard is never over. He is combat ready.

Jerry's soul seeks satisfaction in ownership. He insisted that we live in the country because neighbors are untrustworthy pests, so we bought a small farm. He accumulates every implement ever heard of by the mechanical-minded farmer. Tractors, trailers, hay mowers, bailers, grain grinders, plows . . . he has to have them all! Every time he has an idea for a new piece of machinery he obsesses over it, pores over the classified ads, travels thousands of miles, until he eventually purchases what he wants. Nothing really makes Jerry happy because rust corrodes even the most sophisticated of machinery.

Jerry doesn't take kindly to anyone who gets in the way of him and something he wants. He walks determinedly in his boots, threatening, attacking, and defeating anyone who tries to stand in his way. He knows how to get what he wants. In my visual image of Jerry, he's wearing grease-stained, work-worn logger jeans held up with a pair of wide, stretched-out suspenders. His plaid flannel shirt is torn and reeks of gasoline. His thin, wiry black hair pokes out from under the manure-caked John Deere baseball cap on his small head. He's clanging a wrench against the cold steel innards of his tractor and sandblasting the air with an endless spray of profanity.

The vividness of this writing is achieved, in part, by the selection of verbs: *seeks, insisted, accumulates, obsesses, pores, corrodes, reeks, pokes, clanging, sandblasting.* Verbs are a writer's most potent medium. To learn more about using verbs effectively, turn to chapter 28.

Identify disturbances to your peace. Feel free to write about negative feelings. They are likely not going to be reasonable, and rightly so. Feelings are different from reasons, but they are inarguably real.

List people who have done the following to you:

- Irritated
- Frustrated
- Neglected
- Abused
- Manipulated
- Repressed
- Harmed

Write to one of the following prompts:

- I seethed with turmoil when…
- "I can't take this any more!" I thought when…
- My neck and shoulders tense every time…

Read your rough draft aloud to someone who is supportive and caring, or listen the way an understanding friend would listen, as you read this draft aloud to yourself.

Dave Chavez wrote about how his inner peace was poisoned and also about his response, his determination to "banish the inner demons of doubt, fear, and judgment" within himself. Twenty-five years after recovering from drug abuse, Dave found out he had hepatitis C. He says, "I've often let this legacy of doing intravenous drugs trigger fear and despair. Yet, this and other painful events have also been catalysts that prompted me to search for meaning and see life's preciousness. It also became evident to me that God's grace, those unexpected and unmerited freebies, which help us through difficult times, spare us, and teach us, takes many forms."

> *I made acquaintance with a woman this summer, who wrote me a parting letter, detailing the many faults she saw in me. It was very harsh and judgmental. Among other things, she told me that I was dying from hepatitis C. I found this incredibly insensitive and mean-spirited. She had no specific clues as to my diagnosis. The disease is fatal to a minority of those who have it. Mentally, I rebelled and challenged her assertion, all the while totally aware that I had foreseen visions of death on hundreds of occasions since being diagnosed.*
>
> *I then realized how readily I distance myself from negative doomsayers, but how hard it was to silence my inner critic and nightmare visions. I would have yelled and cursed the presence of anyone who spoke so darkly to me about myself. Truly, I am my own worst enemy. How I wish I could become the inner friend I've always needed.*
>
> *Sometimes when I think of how far I am from where I'd like to be, in terms of my inner qualities and behavior, I cry out, "Dear God, help me banish the inner demons of doubt, fear, and judgment. Teach me gently, to be gentle, positive, and thankful, for I feel there is a great desert in my soul."*

To gather ideas for your second writing, first identify your sources of peace. Peaceful feelings are often associated with our senses. List sensations that soothe your spirit.

The touch of a familiar blanket relaxes young children. You may be refreshed by the feel of summer rain on your skin. List examples of:

- Touch that you find soothing
    - ~ Of a person
    - ~ Of an animal
    - ~ Of natural objects
    - ~ Of furnishings
    - ~ Of tools or musical instruments
    - ~ Of clothing
    - ~ Of weather
- Sounds that soothe you
    - ~ Natural
    - ~ Musical
    - ~ Vocal
    - ~ Mechanical
- Sights that soothe you
    - ~ Out-of-doors
    - ~ At home
    - ~ In public places
- Smells that soothe you
    - ~ From childhood
    - ~ From the present
- Tastes you find soothing
    - ~ Beverages and foods associated with nurturing experiences
- Calming thoughts
    - ~ Memories
    - ~ Passages from literature
    - ~ Poems
    - ~ Prayers

If you are writing with companions, share your list with a partner. You're certain to gain ideas from your partner's list.

Some of us invite inner peace through the practice of personal rituals. We usually go to a quiet place apart from work activities and move into a space of time outside of tight schedules and pressing deadlines. The physical body is stilled first. Breathing deepens and slows. Gradually the mind becomes quiet.

When we pray, we are likely to focus on things in their individuality. When we meditate, we may try to release all thoughts so that strengths and calm present in ourselves can emerge—and so that strengths and calm beyond ourselves can be felt.

> *Be still and know that I am God.*
>
> —PSALM 46:10

Many people find peace through certain activities. At the end of a cross-country ski trek, an acquaintance commented, "I didn't realize until we got back to the car that all the way into the lake and back, I was praying." His body was tired, but his mind was at peace. Prayer may be unfocused as well as focused.

Ordinary chores can provide moments of peace: slipping one's hands into sudsy, warm water to wash dishes; weeding a garden; polishing a car; delivering meals to elderly people; rocking or reading to a young child.

Noncompetitive communal activities frequently bring a sense of peace through harmony. They range from singing in a choir or crewing on a river to cooking in a soup kitchen, constructing housing for homeless people, assisting with disaster relief, and joining volunteers who pick up litter. Peace sometimes springs from humble, mundane sources.

List the rituals and activities through which you find peace.

Exchange lists with a partner. Notice how your lists are similar and different.

Write about a time or times when you have experienced inner peace. You may prefer to write about a particular occasion when you were filled with great calm, or you could write about the sources of peace that reoccur in your life.

Dana Furgerson teaches special education classes at a middle school and a high school in which her students have physical, intellectual, or emotional disabilities. At the end of her teaching day, Dana changes into her running clothes and lets her body outrace her mind. In the evenings she writes; and, as you will see here, she also gardens.

> *Gardening saves me from myself. Throughout my life, my gardens have given me refuge and tranquility. I tend my garden and fall into myself and my imaginings. I find my soul's roots in my garden.*

The smell of damp earth, chicken manure, and decayed flowers' stems and bean vines opens windows to my ancestral heritage of farmers in Ireland and Rumania. In my mind's eye, I see them stooped over rows of cabbages and turnips. They gauge how many hours of fieldwork they have left in the day and what they must finish by dark. My garden becomes my survival, as gardens have always been for my ancestors. I tend, gather, and harvest in anticipation of the coming winter.

My soul opens to the Earth. My anxieties drain from me. What I should have done or shouldn't have done are of no import here in the garden. All that matters is balance. I am the gardener. I provide the care and nourishment to help my plants flourish.

I sing as my hands grasp, weed, and yank. I study the progress of vegetables as I murmur childhood rhymes. My fingers, hands, and arms are smeared in dirt, streaked with pungent dandelion, and pricked and bleeding. At such times, if asked, I would say yes, leave me stay in my garden forever.

Lost memories come to me and linger. I treasure them, analyze them, grieve them, and giggle over them. Grandma Lupei, in her garden, works by my shoulder. The over-grown crooks and crannies of my garden become those of hers and my child self wanders there on sunny summer days. Raspberries, strawberries, blueberries, grapes—the sweet-ness fills my head, and I am again the child gorging herself on berries, warm, full, happy.

Creatures abound in my gardens. Earthworms come for all the humus. Raccoons come for the earthworms. Bugs come to my plants. Garter snakes come for the bugs. Slugs come for the moisture and plants. Chickadees, nuthatches, and robins come for the seeds and worms. Bees come for the pollens. My favorite, the bumblebee, lumbers from plant to plant, the perfect serene gatherer.

Whole days go by as I work and my mind wanders to my childhood, my mar-riages, my son, and my job. All assume serenity when I'm in my garden. Life follows a rhythm in the garden. Rebirth follows loss. Care and devotion yield harvest. Sun heats my back and rain drizzles it. I balance my life in the garden.

Find a peaceful time and a place where you can read your rough draft aloud. Gently and appreciatively listen to yourself. Take note of the ways you have found peace, and consider ways you can cultivate yet more inner calm.

As you hear the drafts of your fellow writers, listen to discover paths new to yourself that you too could follow.

Mary Ann Klausner is a counselor in practice in Eugene, Oregon. She writes in her memoirs about how she finds inner peace after listening to the turmoil and troubles of clients.

I spend hours each day listening to the sorrows, confusion, longings, and life dreams of clients who sit in my presence exploring and questioning their next life steps. They search for purpose and meaning, connection and creativity.

I listen from my soul and mind and body as they reflect on their life experiences, childhood, adolescent, young and middle adulthood. I am impressed with their sincerity, their courage to unearth the pebbles, to describe the currents of their own life river. I witness the integration and joy they often discover in their everyday lives, the bumps and bruises along the way, the faith they show in including me on their journey.

Yet the silence I seek to do the same type of reckoning often eludes me. Five children are now grown and gone. The home in nature, built on stilts, has now turned into a tiny cottage condominium with great windows, white freshly painted walls, a front deck holding pots of geraniums and morning glories. The television has been sold, the stereo is turned off. The telephone is rarely answered as I seek my own internal voice, the voice so many others have attempted to change through the years. I hear the crickets chirping out my bedroom window and glance at the stars and moon as they sit in the night sky. My interior voice is "growing louder, more insistent," and I remain committed to listen and honor it. Fifty-seven years' worth of experience, observations, perceptions, and curiosity have contributed echoes of sound, bouncing off the inside wall of my spirit, requesting my time and attention.

Write paragraphs in response to the following suggestions and questions:

- Describe frustrations or turmoil you suffered that later resulted in peace.
- Has the distress you experienced made you stronger? If so, how?
- Where did you find comfort? Consolation? Liberation?
- What internal qualities enabled you to overcome the turmoil?
- What people have shown you the way to inner peace?
- When have you felt in harmony with your surroundings?
- Describe any occasions when you had a sense of completeness.
- What philosophies or beliefs have guided you to peace?
- Tell about any time when you felt yourself in union with God.

When you write your final drafts, you might like to add photographs, copies of prayers, clippings, souvenirs, articles, or any other memorabilia that illustrates your writing.

Support us, Lord, all the day long,
until the shadows lengthen, and the evening comes,
the busy world is hushed, the fever of life is over, and our work done;
then Lord, in your mercy, give us safe lodging,
a holy rest and peace at the last.

—A NEW ZEALAND PRAYER BOOK
Book of the Anglican Church in Aotearoa, New Zealand, Polynesia

CHAPTER 22

Dreams and Visions

*The dream is the small hidden door
in the deepest and most intimate sanctum of the soul,
which opens into that primeval cosmic night
that was soul long before there was a conscious ego
and will be soul far beyond what a conscious ego could ever reach.*

—CARL GUSTAV JUNG
Swiss psychiatrist

IF YOU ARE ATTENTIVE to your dreams, you'll find this chapter a potent medium toward understanding and revealing the emotions that underlie your conscious life. Even though you may be able to recall and write about only fragments of your dreams, those remembered, elusive, incomplete segments can provide insights into your soul. If, however, your acquaintance with your dreams is sparse you may prefer to skip this chapter.

Dreams and visions may come while we sleep or meditate, or whenever we are relaxed and receptive. Powerful dreams and visions sometimes appear to us during illnesses and catastrophes, and people have reported experiencing especially vivid dreams while they were anaesthetized.

From ancient times to the present, the importance of dreams has been recognized. Their symbolic language is credited with prophesying the future, revealing the present, and explaining the past. Behind our conscious minds we discover unrecognized fears, wild happiness, and revelations about relationships.

In revealing our dreams we expose an unguarded part of ourselves. Honor your own dreams and the dreams of other writers. Dreams that appear to be nonsense may symbolically represent our psychological state. Absurd-seeming dreams may have underlying meaning and significance. Listen gently to all dreams, as they may be profoundly insightful and come from emotions deep within the dreamer.

Use one of the following prompts to write about a dream you had while sleeping or a vision you had while conscious. Write quickly without concern for accuracy.

- An especially vivid dream I remember…
- A recurrent dream I've had…
- A dream that awakened me was…

Recognizing that dreams are often macabre, irreverent, absurd, or even obscene, be prepared to accept your dream without embarrassment. Read your dream aloud to yourself or to anyone you know who is interested in dreams and accepting of the uncensored, subconscious mind.

If you are writing with fellow writers, find a partner and read your dream accounts to each other.

Ask your listener not to judge you by your dream and to acknowledge that you are not responsible for what you dreamed.

A Critical Listening Variation

Listeners should respond only by asking the writer what the dream might mean. Listeners should not presume to interpret the dream.

Gather ideas for more writing. Make brief notes about dreams, visions, or recurrent daydreams that did any of the following:

- Frightened you
- Reflected struggle with a destructive power
- Surprised you
- Were about something or someone you had forgotten
- Were telepathic, communicating with the mind of someone else by extra-sensory means

- Were clairvoyant, allowing you to discern objects not present to your senses
- Were prophetic or indicated foreknowledge
- Were synchronistic (coinciding with another event without causal relationship to one another, sometimes an inner event, such as a dream corresponding with external reality)
- Solved a problem
- Occurred when you were delirious
- Occurred when you were near death or felt near death
- Took you outside of your body
- Brought someone to you who had previously died or departed
- Were interactions with a higher source: a superior part of yourself or an external response to your need for help or clarity
- Used metaphors or symbols to illustrate your situation

We are sometimes approached through nonvisual senses. You may have heard a person who was not physically present speak to you, or you may have sensed an invisible hand on your shoulder. A woman whose husband died several years ago reports occasionally smelling fresh whiffs of his cigar in their home. If you have had a similar, nonvisual experience, make notes about it at this time.

Relating half-forgotten dreams helps return them to consciousness. Find a comfortable setting where you can forget your surroundings and look inward. With half-closed eyes, describe everything you can remember, accepting that your telling may be incoherent and incredible.

Though your dream or vision may be incomplete and seem unintelligible, you are ready to write about it. Don't attempt to make sense of it. Simply try to include as many details as possible. Include all your senses that were affected: sight, hearing, touch, smell, and taste.

Tell how the dream made you feel.

John Pierce, minister of Westminster Presbyterian Church in Eugene, Oregon, related the following dream experience in his memoirs. As a young man John had intended to become a physician, so his undergraduate major was biology. He says, "Being raised in a highly critical home and educated in the scientific method has made me skeptical of my own experience. Maybe that is not all bad. Discernment must take place. That experience of Uncle Earl [described in my memoirs] was the beginning of the numinous dreams I began having in my life and over which I have no control."

Along toward morning I had a dream. (There are occasions when dreams in Old Testament Writ are termed "night visions.") I dreamed I saw Uncle Earl lying on his bed. As I observed him I saw a figure in radiant white enter the room and step to the foot of the bed. I could not see his face but knew it was Jesus, though I cannot say how I knew. This radiant One reached out his hand, took Earl's hand, and pulled him forth from his body. It seemed as if the "real" Uncle Earl emerged from what had been the Uncle Earl I knew.

I sat up wide awake and startled. Taking a deep breath, I lay back down thinking that it's "just a dream. Go back to sleep." I knew my uncle was dying and this must be the workings of my subconscious churning in my sleep. In no more than two minutes, while lying in bed trying to calm myself, the phone rang. Early morning light peeked through the east window. My Aunt Margaret called to say that Uncle Earl had just died and she thought we would want to know.

Read your account aloud and marvel at the ingenuity of your subconscious.

This time exchange rough drafts and listen while your account is read by someone else. This act of distancing may help you to better understand your vision or dream. As you listen, visualize your dream as you would a fantastic tale told to you. Watch for symbols and motifs. Look at your dream as something apart from yourself.

Listen to dreams of other writers with readiness to marvel at the mind of the visionary.

Elaine S. Rudolph wrote the following entry as part of her "spiritual healing journey" while undergoing chemotherapy for lung cancer. During a meditation, two spirit guides came to her in the form of large birds like snowy egrets. Their eyes were compassionate and loving. "I call them my teachers or my helpers," she explained.

I hadn't thought about my Healing Temple for years. It had seemed somehow… outdated. I'd constructed it in my mind thirty years ago. It was—is—beautiful.

I gaze fondly at my glistening, white marble temple, taking in every detail: its perfect roundness, the arched entryway at the top of five stairs, the two luminous pillars on either side of the entrance. I can't see it yet but a large, translucent dome is the heart of my healing temple. Through the dome's portal beams a column of intensely bright, white light. It illuminates my marble healing table. Well do I know this healing Light! It is divine, unconditional Love.

I yearn to be in my temple again…and of course here I am, climbing the steps with my helpers. We pass between the entry pillars and walk across the white tiled floor to my healing table. Reverently I place my hand on its cool, polished surface, remembering the unlikely, wonderful way it conforms to my body. So many times have I lain here and received healing. I glance at my teachers.

"Not yet, Elaine." Their voices speak as one while their long beaks reach toward me. With curiosity and awe, I realize…yes, their beaks are painlessly penetrating my body to withdraw the tumor.

"Corruption cannot survive the Light," they say softly as they place a small, dark mass on the table. I watch in fascination as the white light changes the ugly lump, ever so slowly, into a tiny pile of dry, gray powder that wafts away in the Light.

"It's gone," I say in wonder, knowing with absolute certainty it is gone for good. "Now is your time on the table," they say, turning to me.

I'm lying comfortably on my cool, marble table. A bird teacher is on each side. I feel anticipation and joy. They lean toward me and their long beaks gently touch my skin. They are reaching inside my body with their long tongues to remove all remaining cancer cells. They carefully probe every cubic millimeter of my body. I understand when their search is complete and slide off the table to watch. Two long, sleek beaks carefully place minute black dots into the Light. They become airy and waft away.

My bird helpers' gentle eyes hold mine. "Your healing is complete, but you must continue to take good care of your body, Elaine. Your body has become weakened and needs time to rebuild. Remember, the body's clock runs slower than the spirit's clock." I nod. Yes, I need to be reminded of this. It will take longer for my cure to become apparent to others.

Once in a while a dream's meaning is readily apparent, but reflection on most dreams yields further understanding. Take time to consider the following questions:

- What images do you find in your dream?
- How might you interpret the images symbolically?
- What kinds of kinship or connectedness do you see reflected?
- Some dream analysts think our dreams compensate for our conscious attitudes. Because the ego has a limited perspective, the dream compensates by saying,

"What about this?" The dream adds to our understanding to give us a whole picture. Has any one of your dreams functioned in this way?

- If your dream or vision suggests a parable, a short story that illustrates a truth or teaching, interpret it.
- Can you construe a personal myth from your dream or vision? Can the components of your dream be seen as symbols for your life as a whole?
- Explain how your vision does or does not offer solace and reassurance.

To scrutinize a powerful dream can be disturbing. If writing about your dream causes you to feel overwhelmed, consider talking with a counselor who has been trained in dream analysis.

Revise your rough drafts if you wish to add thoughts. Give them titles, and proofread them for mechanical correctness. Write final drafts on acid-free paper.

Most dreams appear to be enacted on the stage of our soul to teach us something. If we understand the dream, we can often recognize some of the forces at work in our lives and decide which direction we should move in.

—MORTON KELSEY
Episcopal priest
Professor, Notre Dame University

CHAPTER 23

Encountering the Numinous

To Mercy, Pity, Peace, and Love
All pray in their distress;
And to these virtues of delight
Return their thankfulness.

—William Blake
English poet and painter

THE NUMINOUS is that which we perceive to be holy or divine. Our accounts of contact with the numinous reveal the pure flame of our souls, for in the presence of that which is sacred to us we shed pretense and ego and discover our essence.

Individuals perceive the numinous in different ways. There is no one correct definition of sacred experience because, by definition, holiness is beyond comprehension. In this chapter you'll write about an experience of profound meaning that goes beyond rational understanding.

The writer of the following account grew up on a farm in Europe just before World War II. She has studied and worked in both Europe and the United States. At the time of this writing, she said, "I have known, loved, lost remarkable regular people and, now retired, write to tell our stories and what I learned."

An outsized event, the most amazing thing, one of those rare times when one is a
direct witness to the miracle of life. One moment there was my body, large and aware

of work being done inside it, of movements completely separate from my volition. But nothing could prepare me for the next experience, of looking at a person who never existed before and yet without whom the universe from now on was inconceivable. I saw the power of the incarnation of the life force and felt blessed, humble, and grand for having been the conduit for this manifestation of the great mysteries.

Even more delicious, it was a real baby with a strong small body, a little girl whose face eerily resembled mine, black hair curling on her head, which a nurse had shaped in "a little curl in the middle of her forehead." She felt compact, resilient in her fragility, content to be. Her eyes in those first few days were the color of oysters, before turning dark, but already she had the steady, curious gaze I still love so much. She ate well and complained when she was hungry. That got me in trouble for a while as I could not resist her cries, fed her too often, and got us both on an insane two-hour nursing schedule which exhausted both of us until I had the painful courage to let her cry so we could both fully rest between larger feedings.

I knew then that I would truly give my life for her if it was called for. I never would be so amazed, enthralled, and grateful for the immense power of life.

This time, you'll first gather ideas.

Some of the ways we encounter the numinous, that which is sacred, are through our experiences with people, performing certain rituals or arts, perceptions in particular places. Chronicle times when you felt close to the divine.

- Take notes on people through whom you have sensed the numinous
  - ~ People who embodied extraordinary compassion
  - ~ Someone of any age who elicited unexpected goodness in yourself
  - ~ Mentors who guided you
  - ~ Someone who appeared to you in an apparition or dream
- List places that feel holy
  - ~ Out-of-doors places
  - ~ A place of worship
  - ~ An unlikely place where, to your surprise, you sensed the presence of God
- Cite practices that have brought you into contact with the numinous
  - ~ A particular prayer or time of prayer
  - ~ Meditation
  - ~ Religious sacraments
  - ~ Creative work
  - ~ Music

    ~ Sports, dance, or exercise

    ~ Art

    ~ Expressions of love in all forms and relationships

    ~ Poetry and literature

- List animals or objects that conveyed the numinous

    ~ A pet or wild animal

    ~ A tree or plant

    ~ A relic or holy object or memento

    ~ A symbol or light

- Identify events not rationally explained involving:

    ~ An intuition for which no rational explanation is apparent

    ~ A voice

    ~ A moment of heightened awareness

    ~ A time of radical amazement

    ~ A burst of joy

    ~ A dream

    ~ Mental or physical healing

    ~ The presence of someone, or some being, from afar

From your chronicle choose the subject ripe with energy, the one that feels most important to you, or the one that draws you. Some writers have identified a theme, such as music, under which they tell about numerous particular experiences.

Explain what was going on in your life at the time of your experience. Give background. Dare to confide what you might not state in public. After you've finished writing, you can decide whether to voice what you have written or leave it quietly on the page.

Possible ways of beginning this draft are:

- When I was…
- Whenever I hear (see, smell, touch)… I remember…
- The most extraordinary event occurred when…

Pat Vallerand calls herself a "recovering attorney." After seventeen years of practicing law, she found the courage to quit her practice and embark on a journey that has involved self-discovery, learning to live peacefully with the chronic pain of fibromyalgia, and unearthing feelings buried long ago in order to succeed in a very competitive and adversarial profession. Here is her account of a hike with her friend, Cheryl, along the shores of Waldo Lake in Oregon's Cascade Mountains.

On this occasion we were walking on the west shore in a vast forest of majestic old growth firs. Below the gently swaying branches, the feet of these stately giants were carpeted in the striking green of moss and ferns. As we walked along in quiet companionship, I had an experience that I had never had before—and haven't had since.

It was a partially cloudy day, although dry. Not too hot, not too cold. The clouds were high and filmy. Clearly not thunderheads. Yet there was a feeling of energy, of electric charge, in the air. It seemed to be coming from the trees. I had the strong sense that the trees were trying to reach out to me—to communicate something that was important for me to know.

I also felt the energy within myself. At least "energy" seems like the best way to describe it. I felt filled with power. Not the kind of power I had ever felt before—not like the power I have often felt in my work as a lawyer, taking over a courtroom to fight for my client's rights. A very different kind of power. This was a healing, loving power. I felt it rising up in me, as if it was being poured down through the crown of my head into my feet and filling my entire body. I felt lighter, happier, and brimming with intense love; both love flowing into me and love flowing out. I felt compelled to exclaim (through my thoughts), "I love you" to all the trees and plants surrounding me. And I heard them respond—the trees and plants were telling me that they loved me as well.

I reached my hands out, palms up, and felt joy and love emanating into and out of them. There was so much intense energy I was afraid that if I actually touched something, sparks would fly.

I quietly described what I was experiencing to Cheryl, and we walked on in silence, enveloped in this love and energy. I felt as if I were floating. Colors and smells were intensified. I don't know how long we went on like this. In some ways, it seemed so brief, in other ways, the time seemed endless. I think we walked about a mile in this aura.

Why? What was the message I was to receive from this experience?

I have thought about that day many times since. It seems that what I was meant to learn was how to really accept love, to know that I am truly lovable as I am, and to know that the universe is safe, kind, and compassionate. Having felt that love and compassion, I can know that all experiences in life are ultimately positive. And, even more importantly, I can pass on that message to others, by conveying that love to everyone and everything I come in contact with.

When we accept the universe's love and allow it to flow through us, we become connected with each other and everything around us. In this connection we become the One—the spirit of life; there are no differences, nothing to judge. When we become the One, we are able to truly see the "forest." We are able to see that ultimate good comes from every experience.

You may be eager to share what you have written with people you know, or you may prefer to keep it to yourself. Let your feelings and inclinations be your guide. If you wish to read your rough draft to listeners, give them this advice:

"Many of us seldom speak of our encounters with the numinous because they go beyond scientific ways of understanding contemporary life. We fear we would be ridiculed if we related our experiences, so we guard our noncognitive knowledge in our hearts.

"As you listen to my account, set aside all skepticism. You are privileged to hear what can be confided only to a true friend. Withhold your own interpretation or explanation."

> *Negative capability, that is, when a man is capable of being in uncertainties, mysteries, doubts, without any irritable reaching after fact and reason…*
> —JOHN KEATS
> English poet

Geraldine H. Crawford was working as a substitute teacher in Detroit, Michigan, when her adult son, Doug, was shot to death.

> *No! It couldn't be! His body was there, but Doug wasn't there—that effervescent spirit, that curious and adventuresome boy who was always on the go, that compassionate person who was always helping someone and cheering people up, that raconteur who could tell me of his comic adventures now that he was thirty. I almost physically recoiled from the quiet stillness of his body and left the hospital room where it was. I murmured, "He is not there."*
>
> *A chaplain was waiting for me outside the door. I began talking and talking incessantly to him, but I don't remember a word of what I said.*
>
> *I finally left and found my car. Although the school policeman had driven me to the hospital, I drove home alone, but I couldn't stand being at home alone so I got into the car to go somewhere. . . . I decided to go to Doug's home. He and his friend Cliff were both social workers for Wayne County. They had bought the house and had planned to fix it up and make some money on it with their own hard work. I knocked and was let in. Several of Doug's friends and his recent girlfriend were sitting glumly around the living room. Some were drinking soft drinks and others beer—and then I spied the blood on the wall and the door leading outside. I knew immediately that it was my son's blood. He had given it willingly for a baby of a friend who had needed it, but NOT THIS violent act! All I wanted to do was leave as soon as possible.*

I got to my car. That blood was Doug's. It had struck me with almost physical force. I fled in my car down the street, and as I did I looked up and there was Doug! He said, "I understand, Mom. I understand!" To this day, I believe it was his spiritual self speaking from his heart to me.

Do not feel that you must be able to explain your encounter with the numinous. The numinous is defined as ineffable, or beyond our understanding. Mystery is inherent. We describe, rather than explain, such realities.

Make notes as you reflect on the following suggestions. Your responses are likely to help you to tell about your experience more fully.

- If you transcended your usual limitations, tell what happened.
- Were mercy, pity, peace, or love aspects of your experience?
- Describe your spiritual empowerment.
- If you experienced divine presence, describe your perception of it as best you can.
- Numinous experiences are often said to be outside of time. What was the time frame of your experience?
- If you reached beyond yourself to unite with others, describe how you felt in the dimension you entered.

At this time you've probably written only one rough draft, but you accumulated ideas for other drafts by listing times when you felt close to the divine. Write additional drafts from ideas you chronicled, or place that list in your greenhouse file.

You have revealed much of your individuality, your deepest feelings, your soul.

Miracles seem to rest,
not so much upon faces or voices or healing power
coming suddenly near to us from far off,
but upon our perceptions being made finer
so that for a moment our eyes can see and our ears can hear
that which is about us always.

—WILLA CATHER
American author

CHAPTER 24

Spiritual Well-Being

Grandfather,
Look at our brokenness.

We know that in all creation
Only the human family
Has strayed from the Sacred Way.

We know that we are the ones
Who are divided
And we are the ones
Who must come back together
To walk in the Sacred Way.

Grandfather,
Sacred One,
Teach us love, compassion, and honor
That we may heal the earth
And heal each other.

—Prayer of the Ojibway Nation
A people indigenous to North America

SPIRITUAL WELL-BEING does not necessarily correspond with our physical, economic, or social well-being. It's true that health of body and mind are linked and that physical health is affected by economic prosperity. However, all the facets of ourselves are interrelated, and spiritual health may, or may not, track with other ups and downs. Sometimes spiritual growth quickens when we struggle on other fronts.

As you gather ideas you'll chart different aspects of your well-being from your childhood to your present age. But first, warm up to writing.

Choose one of the following prompts or create your own:

- A time when I had a sense of well-being in spite of difficult circumstances was when…
- My spirit was low when…
- My spiritual life intensified when…

One writer, Cheryl Roffe, began her rough draft this way:

> *One of the worst times of my life gave me one of the greatest spiritual gifts I have ever received. I remember getting up early on a cold March morning to have my meditation time before work. It was a gray, dripping, gloomy world outside, which reflected precisely what was going on inside me. I was terribly afraid because everything seemed to be going wrong in my life, and I already felt that the world was a grim place, full of pain and crisis.*
>
> *As I sat on the couch in the little den that I used for meditation each morning…*

From this beginning, Cheryl related an experience that ended with her being "suddenly flooded with light, warmth, and a sense of well-being." At a time when major things were going wrong in her life, she arrived at a state of "quiet, intense bliss." Cheryl was spiritually very well in spite of what was happening to her, but the opposite can, and often does, happen. Your story might show either parallels or divergences between certain circumstances in your life and your spiritual well-being.

If you've written about a time you're glad to remember, it may involve someone with whom you are still in contact. If so, telephone that person and read this draft to him or her. If you prefer to mail it, read it aloud to yourself first and then write and mail a copy.

If you're no longer in contact with companions from the time you described, read this draft aloud to a young person, someone who will glimpse a dimension of you you've not previously shown.

If you are writing with colleagues, read your drafts to each other.

When you are ready to revise this draft, reenter the experience you described by using the technique in chapter 4. While remembering and reconstructing the drama you felt, you'll be able to add a sense of presence and dimension to your final version.

> *Adversity reveals genius, prosperity conceals it.*
>
> —HORACE
> Roman poet, 65–68 BCE

Gather ideas for your next draft by charting aspects of your life. Look at the graph in figure 10; and then, to make your own, turn a large sheet of paper sideways. Halfway down the page draw a horizontal line across the paper from one edge to the other.

Near the bottom of the page draw another horizontal line. Under it, write numbers in increments of five up to about the age you are now.

If you have colored pencils or pens, choose five contrasting colors to draw five different-colored circles in a row near the top of the page. Give the circles the following labels: "physical," "economic," "social/cultural," "vocational/professional," and "spiritual/emotional." You'll use the corresponding colors to chart different aspects of your life on the graph.

The following directions will be helpful.

PHYSICAL

Think of the horizontal line across the midstrip of the graph as indicating average. If your physical well-being was below average when you were fifteen years old, place your mark below average at age fifteen. Use the color you placed in the physical well-being circle to indicate your health. When you had excellent physical health, bring the line above average. Your line will dip when you suffered injuries or illnesses and rise when you were in peak condition. Traverse your line across the graph from your earliest memories or knowledge about your health to the age you are now.

ECONOMIC

Now switch pencils or pens to use the color that indicates economic well-being. If your family was economically deprived when you were a child, place your indicator line below average; if your family was affluent, place your line high on the graph. Indicate your economic well-being throughout your life.

Economic well-being and the other categories are relative to personal expectations and experience. Your narrative, not the graph, is what will tell your story. If your family had few consumer goods but ate wholesome food, was adequately clothed and sheltered, and felt well-off, your written interpretation could explain any disparity between your placement on economic income charts and your sense of material well-being. For

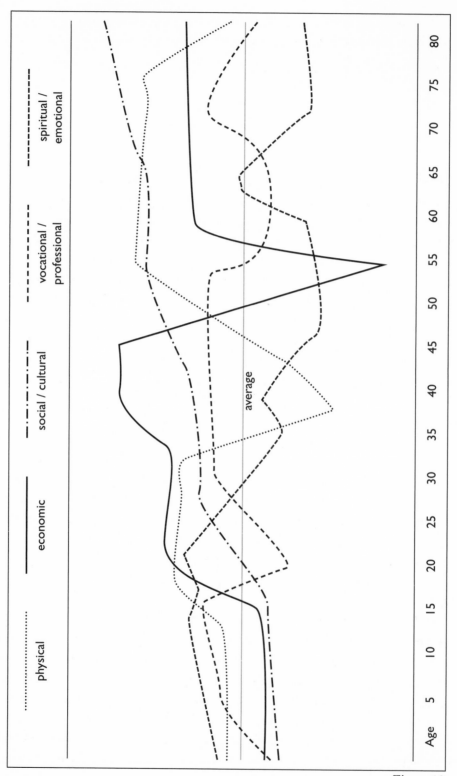

Figure 10

purposes of the perspective you'll gain from filling in this graph, mark your graph as objectively as possible, knowing it is only a device to prompt your writing.

SOCIAL/CULTURAL

Interpret the terms used on the graph according to whatever the words *social* and *cultural* mean to you. Define them for yourself. If you love going to baseball games and socializing at tailgate picnics and you have been privileged to enjoy many games and picnics, place your line high on the graph. Attainment of the educational and social goals you set belong here too. This category also includes volunteer activities.

If you were often without friends or unable to take part in cultural activities, lower your line. Any manner in which you mark your graph is probably going to require written explanation. For example, if you were a student abroad living on a small stipend, you might have had few friends and been too poor to attend cultural events. However, the experience of living abroad would be rich in immersion in a new culture, so you would write about that complexity.

VOCATIONAL/PROFESSIONAL

When you chart this category, use the pencil or pen with which you colored the vocational/professional circle. Your childhood vocation was probably to be a student along with some added responsibilities. Your adult vocation might be the rearing of children and caring for members of your family.

Whether your analysis is subjective or objective doesn't matter as long as your writing tells how your work affects your well-being and how you feel about it. If, as a teenager, you had a job you considered good for someone under twenty, place your graph line high, but if you held a similar job at an older age when you wanted different employment, move the graph line down. Again, you will have the dilemma of deciding whether to place your mark according to external criteria or your own feelings. You could consider certain work excellent because you loved doing it, even though it didn't pay well; and conversely, you may give a low ranking to lucrative work you disliked.

SPIRITUAL/EMOTIONAL

Use your personal beliefs to define spiritual/emotional well-being. If desired, you could chart them separately.

Begin by writing a list on another sheet of paper on which you name the times in your life when you were powerfully attuned to such things as:

- Intuition
- Passion for knowing
- Drive to do important work

- Inspiration
- Insight
- Imagery
- Meditation
- Silence
- Inner vivacity
- Archetypes, or typical images and associations, motifs
- Values
- Motivation
- Body wisdom
- Imagination
- Wonder
- Compassion

Include times when you felt:

- In communion with strength greater than yourself
- Lifted beyond yourself
- Filled with benevolence for all living things

Some writers evaluate their spiritual well-being from the perspective of a particular religion, while other writers follow their individual sense of the meaning of the word *spiritual*. Chart this subject in a way that corresponds with your own thoughts and feelings.

> *There's a spirituality that's a part of dance that I think I've been able to create. I don't go to church, but I have beliefs and I think that comes across in my dancing. I believe in God. It sounds sort of corny, but a lot of my inspiration comes from my spirituality. Sometimes it does feel like there is something that takes over my body. I'm not a different person when I dance, but I definitely go to a different level of existing.*
>
> —YVONNE BORREE
> New York City Ballet

A good way to consider your spiritual well-being in relation to other aspects of your life is to see where the spiritual/emotional graph line deviates from or parallels other lines. Ask yourself what the graph indicates. Some individuals have said their spiritual lives intensified and strengthened during difficulties, even calamities, while others have become dispirited at such times. Disappointment and grief can sap one's spirit. A chemical imbalance in one's body can rob spiritual vibrancy. Look at what else was happening in your life physically, culturally, economically, and vocationally when your spirit dipped and when it rose.

Carpenters use an instrument called a "spirit level" to ensure that the framework of their construction is plumb.

> *spirit level—An instrument for adjusting any deviation from the horizontal or perpendicular by reference to the position of a bubble of air in a tube of alcohol or other liquid.*
> —BRITANNICA WORLD LANGUAGE DICTIONARY

Your writing probably won't mention your graph at all. If you gained insights from the chart, then it has served its purpose. You can choose to write about your spiritual well-being by telling about a certain significant stage in your life or by explaining how your spiritual life has changed over time.

Begin this draft any way you wish. Here are possible prompts:

- As I look back at different periods of my life, I see that…
- A time when I was spiritually strong though other aspects of my life…
- Over the years my spiritual life has…
- A way I now cultivate my spiritual life is…

Writer and poet Gail Winter wrote the following account while she was working on a book of poetry and prose chronicling her recovery from cancer.

> *We raised the kids with a little bit of both religions. Hanukkah candles and Santa Claus. Dreidels and Christmas trees. It was superficial spirituality. Religion without soul. And I knew it and pretended not to care. I was so conflicted about my own beliefs that it was truly the best I could offer my children.*
>
> *All that changed dramatically with the first cancer diagnosis almost eight years ago. I remember coming home wanting to pray, but not remembering how. The prayers I had learned as a child felt woefully inadequate. I also felt hypocritical. So I sat cross-legged and repeated affirmations and visualized the cancer being eaten alive by Pac Man–type creatures. I eventually started meditating but didn't have a clue as to how to listen. So instead, I started visiting psychics. I was sure they could give me the answers I so desperately craved. I didn't know it then, but I see now that I was looking for the God I had turned my back on in my youth.*
>
> *But there were no easy answers. I continued to grapple with my inner divinity, testing God, wanting proof of her existence. It has been a process of surrendering*

again and again to the mystery. I continue to question, as the cancer has returned a second and third time, why I am still alive and well. Have I won some sort of macabre jackpot? Is the gold in my body? A gold I was blind to? I hear the tinkle of coins and I know what? Nothing. I still have more questions than answers.

But there is a serenity today, a peace I have never felt before. It is a peace fought for on the battleground of my body. It fills my body and spills out onto the landscape of my life. It is what I now refer to as God.

To hear your rough draft, find a place of repose where, as you read, you can listen to the quiet wisdom from within yourself. Resolve to reserve time to do what nourishes your spiritual well-being.

Some people have a friend whom they think of as a spiritual advisor. If you have such a friend, read this draft to that person.

Share your insights with your fellow writers.

Write brief, reflective paragraphs in response to the following questions:

• When has the spiritual dimension in your life been most strong?
• What people and beliefs have guided your spirituality?
• What people and experiences have enlivened your sense of selfhood?
• How has your spirituality changed during your lifetime?

Hy Schneider was a poet and short story writer. He applied his talents to a long career in public relations that included planning political campaigns, as well as writing advertising copy. When he retired, he moved from New York to Oregon to live near his son and daughter.

I have been challenged to "write something spiritual," and, being a nonbeliever, I couldn't begin to attempt an intelligent and meaningful reply. Despite my many adventures, I was uncertain about how to search for an answer. There was nothing particularly spiritual about my experience as a soldier. I had five years of army life and found no spiritual clue. I was on a ship that was torpedoed and had been forewarned to "lay flat on the deck or you would be as flat as a country pancake." That was clearly not spiritual. I had a case of ammunition shifted from a huge truck to my inadequate shoulders, and its weight drove me into the wet ground like a tent peg, with no idea of my having had a spiritual experience of any kind.

However, the answer to my question was within me. My five-year-old daughter, who was then and will always be the apple of my eye, invited me to attend a party at her nursery school. We were playing a public game in which my daughter asked a question of me privately, and I would have to reply for all to hear. Her question was, "Do you love me?" and Victoria reached up and put her little hands on my pink cheeks and turned my eyes to her eyes and stared deeply and earnestly into my eyes as she whispered, "Everybody knows!" That's the closest I've come to feeling "spiritual."

CHAPTER 25

Gratitude

Is it so small a thing to have enjoyed the sun,
to have lived light in the spring, to have loved,
to have thought, to have done?

—Matthew Arnold
English poet

GRATITUDE IS A STATE of mind, a point of view determined only partially by our circumstances. Some people who have suffered injustices and deprivation appreciate kindness, beauty, and growing things; while other people who have reason to be grateful exude bitterness and resentment.

Ingratitude is life denying. Gratitude is life affirming. Today your writing will celebrate your life and affirm the person you are.

Begin by gathering ideas that will help you appreciate the person you are. Complete the following prompts with a sentence or paragraph. Move in any order from one to another.

Playful and serious prompts:

- The funny thing about me is…
- The beautiful thing about me is…
- The strong thing about me is…
- The tender part of me is…

> *I will give thanks unto thee, for I am*
> *Fearfully and wonderfully made.*
>
>   —PSALMS 139:14

If you are writing with companions, share what you wrote by listening to everyone's response, taking one topic at a time. Listen to each person read about the funny or odd quality before going on to the beautiful quality. And remember, even delightful readings must not be reported outside your group.

Robert Morgan, a former boxer, guides memoir-writing groups at his home in Gunbarrel, Colorado. The following excerpt is lifted from the latter part of his memoirs, entitled *Autumn Leaves*.

> *I think everyone is born with at least one talent, a gift from that mysterious, mystical, wondrous force we call God. By "talent" I don't mean the dictionary definition, which leans toward the "creative or artistic," but a broader view of talent that might be called "aptitude."*
>
> *The trick for me when I was young was to discover a talent, which turned out to be amateur boxing. Boxing got me an education and on that foundation, everything else that was worthwhile in life.*
>
> *We're lucky if we have parents who encourage us to find our talent, or even one mentor when we're young and floundering around in the world trying to find out who we are and where we're going. I was more than lucky . . . I had a mentor named Bob Gerber, who became a lifelong friend. He was my first boxing coach when I was fourteen. I didn't go to the boxing gym that first time because I thought I had a talent for boxing or because I loved to fight, I went to get out of the house.*
>
> *When I met Gerber I was five foot eight and one hundred and ten pounds of gangly arms and legs, which kept getting tangled up. I worked hard at it, Gerber saw potential that I never saw and stayed with me. He taught me to box, and after I won my first fight and lost the next three and thought about quitting, he loaned me his confidence and I won eighteen out of the next nineteen.*
>
> *After that he wrote letters and got me a four-year boxing scholarship to the University of Wisconsin. He knew I had bad grades and that I didn't like high school, so he conspired with Sister Rose Marie, my English Literature teacher in my last year of high school, to get my grades up. She was tough but inspired me to want to learn—something that stays with me to this day.*

Through my understanding of poetry in her class, she convinced me I could do college-level work. I could hardly believe it. Boxing and poetry, two seemingly disparate moves in a life that was, until then, without inspiration or direction—two moves that changed my life forever.

Gratitude is a fruit of great cultivation; you do not find it among gross people.

—Samuel Johnson
English author

Probe the praiseworthy qualities in yourself so that you can appreciate and express gratitude for them.

The next list of writing subjects is lengthy. Most topics have potential as openings for full chapters. You'll encounter fifteen potent writing prompts, so give yourself a block of time to respond to all of them. Later, you can choose to develop at length the ones that feel charged with significance.

It may be the greatest task we face on earth is to know ourselves.

—Jeanne Murray Walker
American poet

So that your body does not become cramped or strained, allow yourself to stretch and walk around. Writers can be hard at work while taking a stroll or appearing to gaze out a window. Agree upon when to reconvene. You will need an ample amount of time to respond to the following prompts:

- My most loving friend sees me as…
- Something I do well is…
- My greatest strength is…
- A weakness I try to overcome is…
- Eventually, something I would like to accomplish (achieve) is…
- I did something difficult when I…
- I struggle with…
- I'm grieved by…

- My anchor is…
- I find joy…
- If I could make life better for someone, I would…
- I long for…
- I help to bring about social justice when I…
- My ultimate concern is…
- I'm most grateful to…

> *Gratitude takes three forms: a feeling in the heart,*
> *an expression in words, and a giving in return.*
>
> —Proverb

You're now ready to write to affirm the person you have become. Write a poem, letter, or reflection that shows your gratitude. Freely combine ideas you've gathered, adding your further thoughts.

A POEM

If you write a poem, don't try to rhyme. Simply write free verse. List phrases. The lines will be of different lengths. One way to begin your poem is "I am…" For example:

I am a person who
- Tries to…
- Cries when…
- Loves to…
- Cares deeply about…
- Rails against…(list your own additional phrases)

A LETTER

You might prefer to write a letter. So the receiver will remember the relevant details, reiterate the experience you shared.

Bob Morgan kept in touch with his English teacher, Sister Rose Marie. In a letter to me he explained the following:

> *Sister Rose Marie and I became friends and exchanged letters and phone calls through the years. Because of her, I wrote and had published a book I called* Goodbye, Geraldine, *and since then I have sent her different writings. I was particularly happy about one piece I sent her in 2008 when she was ninety-four years old. She wrote back and said that the piece was fine but it had a dangling participle. I had to go to Google to find out what that was. I then looked at the writing. She was right.*

I have found through the years that it is impossible for me to be grateful and depressed at the same time. And I will always be grateful for a nun whose name was Sister Rose Marie. She was not given to coddling...and it got me into college and has helped me through the years. I knew she was always tough and her "dangling participle" comment proved she hadn't lost her edge.

A REFLECTION

When she was a young child, Beverly Wolff Nagle was boarded out with first one family and then another—a life many people might remember with bitterness. As time went by, Beverly became an artist specializing in Chinese brush paintings. Today she and her daughter weave pine needles into fragrant "Beaver Meadow Baskets."

When I was in third grade, I went to live with an older couple, the Richeys, in Drain, Oregon. They had a daughter, Clara, still living at home, who married Phil Burkhart.

I had been there less than six months when Grandma Richey (that's what I called her) died. Was there a funeral? I don't remember. My big worry was what was going to happen to Me. It was decided I would go live with Clara and Phil, the newlyweds.

Phil, a logger, was a very tall, muscular, good-looking, dark-haired man who liked me immediately. The three of us went to live in a logging camp near Cottage Grove, Oregon. There was a bunkhouse for the single men and cabins for the married couples. I remember the sidewalks were wooden planks put down directly on the ground. This was a wonderful place for the many snakes to sun themselves, and I learned to watch for them. They were the regular garden kind, but that black body with the yellow stripe really gave me many a start.

Our place overlooked the coal deck (a huge stack of logs) and the log pond with the yardarm close by. I was not allowed to play anywhere near any of these things. There were no playmates, and I was lonesome.

Some of the loggers' wives would get together at the "real home" of a close-by lady, and they would quilt. They tried to interest me in this activity, and I did try, but my interest soon waned. I had my eye on the very old pump organ. That was such a joy for me, especially to be trusted to play with a valuable item such as this. I spent many an hour trying to play, and my legs would ache after all the effort it took to pump it. I had never had a music lesson, but I had lots of desire. How those wonderful, patient women put up with my attempt at music, along with my singing, I'll never know.

We soon moved to a quicksilver mining camp on top of a mountain—I think it was one of the Bohemia mines. We had a one-bedroom cabin. I slept in the front room on a single cot that also served as a couch. The outhouse wasn't too bad but the path to it was covered with HUGE slugs, and it took a lot of effort to get there without stepping on one of these slimy things. We had the usual thunder mug for middle-of-the-night relief.

There was a big building where the single men slept and ate their meals. I loved to go visit the cook and smell all the good food she put forth.

The schoolteacher lived across from the bunkhouse in a "real" house. She had a big patch of violets. On occasion she would invite me over to pick a bouquet, probably because I was the only girl in camp. I shall always cherish that experience and the wonderful aroma from those dainty purple flowers.

Next door to our cabin was a family of seven, five of which were boys. The only time they wanted to tolerate me was when I had a new supply of marbles. Then we'd play "keeps," and of course all my marbles would be gone—all except my steely I kept for a shooter. It took me a while to realize these kids did not have my better interest at heart, so I gave up on them and played alone. To amuse myself I made mud sculptures. The front porch was built high enough for me to stand under it, and it had beautiful red dirt that was perfect mixed with water to make men, animals, or whatever came to mind. Then I would put my works of art in the sun to dry. Sometimes they would fall apart when dry and other times I had a masterpiece.

Also a source of amusement and hope was fishing. There was a creek close to our cabin that barely had water in it, but it bubbled over moss-covered rocks and made a quiet, comforting tune. It never occurred to me that there wasn't enough water to hold a fish. I would take a long piece of string and bend a straight pin to form a hook and then sit forever in the hope a fish would want to commit suicide. It never happened.

School was a one-room white building with a potbellied stove for heat and room for grades one through six. When nature called we had to hold up one finger for peeing and two fingers for a B.M. I have no idea why, but it was important if you wanted to leave the room.

My lunch bucket was a silver Kayro can with a handle. There was no refrigeration, so almost everything we ate was in a can. Day after day, on the bottom of this wonderful lunch box, was a sandwich of deviled ham—no mayo, no lettuce, no pickle. Sitting on top of the sandwich was either an orange or apple that left a big dent in the center—then came some sort of cookie. There were no air holes and the tight-fitting lid made everything in the can smell like deviled ham. None of the children would trade lunches with me because they knew how awful my lunch smelled. In fact, when I took off the lid to my can, the whole room could smell it. Oh my!

Phil had a Model A type car with a rumble seat and no heater. In the winter, we would wrap up in a blanket. Thank heaven I was small for my age, because it was a real squeeze to get the three of us in the car.

Looking back I always admired them, a couple adjusting to marriage taking on an eight-year-old. At the end of the school year I was shuttled off to another household, but I shall always look upon the two of them as really special people who cared about me and for me, a little crippled girl. Thank you God for people like that!

Share and respond appreciatively to the writings of one another.

To more fully value your life, reflect on your writing. Find a quiet place to reread it. Notice and be grateful for any of the following qualities you find in yourself:

- Hopefulness
- Spunkiness
- Ability to appreciate
- Resilience
- Empathy
- Courage
- Compassion
- Generosity
- Love

> *A thankful heart is not only the greatest virtue,*
> *but the parent of all other virtues.*
>
> —CICERO
> Roman philosopher

PART IV

The Rewards

CHAPTER 26

A Retrospective Overview and Insights

To live content with small means; to seek elegance rather than luxury,
and refinement rather than fashion; to be worthy, not respectable, and wealthy, not rich;
to study hard, think quietly, talk gently, act frankly; to listen to stars and birds,
to babes and sages, with open heart; to bear all cheerfully, do all bravely,
await occasions, hurry never. In a word, to let the spiritual,
unbidden and unconscious, grow up through the common.
This is to be my symphony.

—WILLIAM HENRY CHANNING
American transcendentalist

YOU HAVE TRAVELED from the outer regions of your life, the territories readily visible to your friends and family, to an inner place where you have written about your greatest joys, intense longings, griefs, good intentions, hopes, and prayers. From this place deep within the labyrinth of your being, you'll look out upon your life with insightful perspective.

Before you do further writing, arrange for a quiet time when you reread everything you've written. Bring out all your chapters and parts of chapters, including the seeds of chapters stored in your greenhouse file. As you read, don't edit or proofread; but in an easy, pleasant, comfortable way, savor the fullness of all your writings.

The overview of your chapters will be revealing. You may see patterns in your life and characteristics in yourself of which you had not been aware. Look at the love you have felt and the ways you have expressed it. Notice where you have placed your resources, time, talent, and money. You will observe strivings and strengths in yourself to be appreciated. Take time to muse about your life and the subject of your memoirs, yourself.

As you write this retrospective chapter, you'll survey your life and reveal some of your philosophy and values. Your contemplations may serve as a way of giving closure to your writings. They bring your voyage to its end.

To prepare for this writing, imagine that you have been alone in a tiny space capsule so long that you've lost track of time. You hear nothing; your capsule is controlled by remote means; and your food is a flavorless pabulum. You are with only your thoughts and memories.

If you find the idea of space travel appealing, then imagine a less attractive way of being banished. For example, imagine that you are in isolation in a hospital bed where you are fed through a tube and forbidden to have television, books, or visitors. Day after day passes as you lie waiting to recover.

In your imagined estrangement, what parts of your present life would you miss? Imagine that from your space capsule or hospital bed you long to return home. Make lengthy lists of the many pleasures you now enjoy that you would miss. Like the child at summer camp who whined that she missed the smell of her father's shaving lotion when it was really her father she missed, include associated sensations, as well as the primary things.

List the things you will miss seeing, hearing, touching, smelling, tasting, and experiencing kinesthetically (see figure 11).

When your list is comprehensive, write to the following prompt:

• When I no longer live on earth, I shall miss…

Of course, you may rephrase this prompt. And remember, free verse is always an option once you begin writing.

Holly Reinhard wrote the following poem when she was only fifteen years old. While Holly was schooled at home, she took advantage of writing workshops in Eugene, Oregon, where she lived with her family and dog, Caleb. As you can see, free verse is an option you might choose.

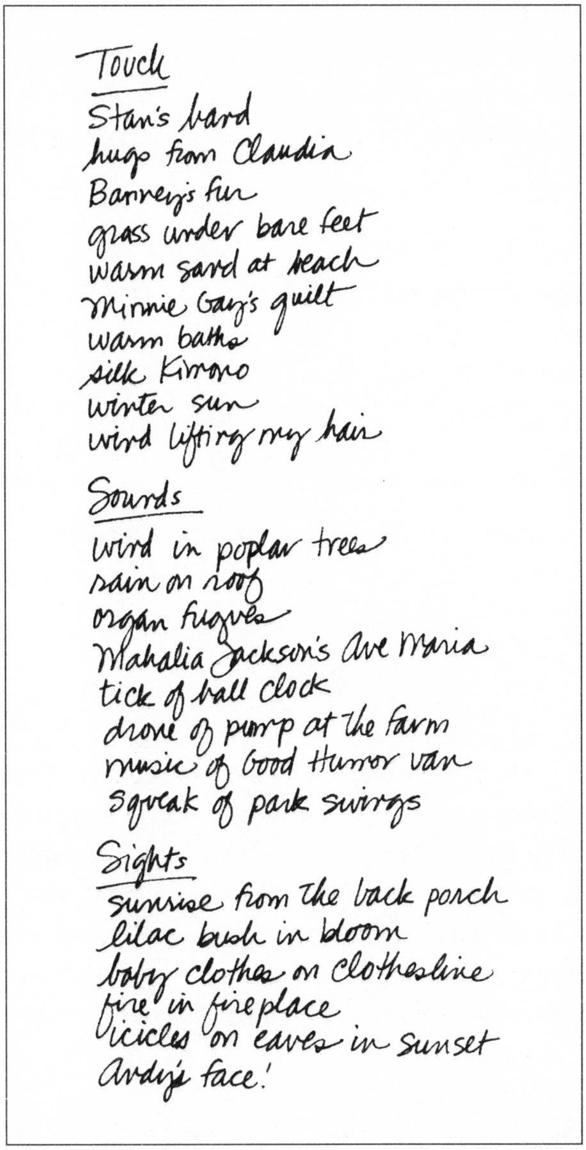

Touch
Stan's beard
hugs from Claudia
Barney's fur
grass under bare feet
warm sand at beach
Minnie Gay's quilt
warm baths
silk Kimono
winter sun
wind lifting my hair

Sounds
wind in poplar trees
rain on roof
organ fugues
Mahalia Jackson's Ave Maria
tick of wall clock
drone of pump at the farm
music of Good Humor van
squeak of park swings

Sights
sunrise from the back porch
lilac bush in bloom
baby clothes on clothesline
fire in fireplace
icicles on eaves in sunset
Andy's face!

Figure 11

When I no longer live on earth
I shall miss
my mom,
Talks we had, her cooking,
The best spaghetti,
Unlike any other spaghetti, with meat and lots of chili powder—
    though not too much.
I shall miss sticking my hand in the

flour when I bake something,
pushing a measuring spoon into the soft powder and making molds.
I shall miss Caleb's mournful
bays and howls at sirens,
his coarse, black fur
silky
from the sun.
I shall miss running outside
in bare feet,
to greet my dad
when he comes home
from work.

Relish your draft as you read it aloud. If you are reading with friends, you'll feast on a banquet of pleasures.

One workshop participant wrote such a poignant catalog of tender moments she will miss that her group advised her to save what she had written to be read after her death at her memorial service. Many people also prepare suggestions regarding music they would like to have played along with favorite verses they would like read at their memorial services. The writer's list showed the people and experiences most meaningful to her and will picture much about who she was if it is read when she eventually dies.

Laura Lyford, like Holly Reinhard, used poetic form. You see here the first line and first stanza of her six-stanza poem.

When I no longer live on this earth, I think that I shall miss:
The alleluia sky of a glorious May morning,
The host of a moon over the Pacific on a warm August night,
The praying arms of oak trees silhouetted against a rainbow sunset,
The grace of bird flocks practicing synchronicity,
The ever-changing colors of nature as day calls out to day
And night to night makes every day unique.

Louise Yawger Cowan began her freshman year in 1932 at Wellesley College, where she became number two on the varsity crew. She found that rowing as a team with seven other women gave her a sense of strength and power, and she loved the early morning call-outs when "the air was always fresh and cool, the campus peacefully burgeoning with spring, and the lake unmarred by a single breeze so that the cox's commands rang out crisp and clear over the water." She wrote this description of an event at twilight.

> *On Float Night there were races between the class crews. Chinese lanterns hung at the bow and stern of each shell, glowing as darkness swept over the lake. At the end of the race all four crews came together to form a giant "W" and sing the alma mater. People watching from the bank sang along, and their voices echoed over the lake to us, resting on our oars in the gathering darkness.*

Many years later, after she was widowed, Louise left her home on the East Coast and moved to Oregon, away from the friends and place she held dear. She told what she missed when she no longer lived in her home.

> *I brought with me from New Jersey memories of days and nights in the little house on Division Avenue, of cold mornings by the fireplace in the kitchen, memories of waking surrounded by the lovely flowered wallpaper in my bedroom, the noises of shaving and song coming from the bathroom, and the snuffling of the little black dog crawling out from under my bed looking for his morning walk.*

Louise's memoirs also show experiences she valued from the time when, as a young woman, she skimmed across the fresh lake in the early mornings to her later years when domestic routines had become most comforting and meaningful.

For your second writing, use many of the following prompts to initiate a series of ruminations:

- In reviewing my life, my biggest surprise is…
- Something I would do differently if I could relive my…
- A satisfaction I have…
- A regret I have…
- My greatest joy has been…
- If necessary, I would have been willing to die for…
- A time when I felt awe (wonder, reverence) was when…
- My overriding concern is…
- I hope my grandchildren…

- My hopes for (name specific people you love) are…
- If I am reincarnated, in my next life I'll…
- I have faith that…

To stimulate thinking and discovery, reflect on your writing. Then actively take notes in response to the following questions:

- With whom or what have I felt union?
- What have I valued in myself?
- What have I valued in other people?
- Have I had a sense of mission?
- What has been my source of illumination?
- When have I felt compassion? Completeness?

Integrate your reflections into your earlier paragraphs or use them as additional musings as you bring your memoirs to a close.

> *What a wonderful life I've had!*
> *I only wish I'd realized it sooner.*
>
> —COLETTE
> French novelist and autobiographer

The following reflection is by Timothy Whitsel, a poet who writes and gardens near Springfield, Oregon, where he lives with his wife, Carol, and three children. For the past four seasons he has directed a monthly program of readings by local writers, The Windfall Reading Series, held in the Eugene Public Library. Notice how Timothy's story moves from the description of a rollicking family meal to his reflections about how we are measured and about grace. This memory and meditation exemplify a splendid final entry.

Falling Grace

There is no implant that will raise a dumb heart to care, to love, to delve. Time and again we must allow ourselves to be drawn in. Attention is no gizmo. Unless we can be lifted, we are old at any age. I know the light kindles in my eyes because I look at you. I do not stop. Set the table. We can eat and have our talk.

My father stood by the table one August evening. I must have been ten or eleven. Days and nights had been muggy, six weeks, without rest. Three boys with lightening bugs and boobs and baseball disappointments on our minds, we would not quiet down for prayer. Mom was frayed. And business anxieties had agitated Dad all summer.

Serving dishes were piled with food: sliced tomatoes and fresh-cooked snapbeans from the garden, corn, pan-braised pieces of round steak. Dad raised his hand for silence. Then sat. As we began to bow, the wooden folding chair, by then advanced in use, creaked like a rusty gate unlocking, and collapsed. Before our half-closed eyes, Dad disappeared. Wrinkles of disbelief exploded on his forehead as he fell.

He never got to pray. Popping up like a dry cork, Dad danced a hootenanny jig to our volcanic laughs. The fartlek howls and giggles did not subside until the food was greasy chilled and night was thick against the window screens. We could not get enough. This is one of my staying memories of home and family and what works, by working not at all. The blessing that came by accident, that night, may happen any time we fall from grace, to grace.

Eternity begins in what we plant and how we tend; in time we all should be so lucky to be overgrown, and, my gut says, we are measured (in the duff) not so much by what or how we change, but rather what we mend. Oh for luck to bless my children so, mending them by my falls and by the alacrity with which I rise to dance. Girls laughing, laughing decades later, laughing when a room seems empty, laughing unstoppably with their dancing fool old man.

If you have been writing with fellow writers, by now you have become intimate associates, bonded in trust and support. Travelers who make geographical tours together often feel a loss of camaraderie when the trip is over; they share addresses and resolve to stay in touch with each other. You who have voyaged together into the realms of your interior lives are likely to feel far more nostalgia as your expedition ends than land and air travelers feel.

Schedule a celebration. Invite each participant to read a selected chapter at your next gathering and to bring food to share.

If you have assembled and bound your final drafts by the time you meet, bring your book to show to one another. Chapter 27 suggests ways to put it together.

The Gift of Yourself

A good book is the precious life-blood of a master spirit,
embalmed and treasured up on purpose to a life beyond life.

—JOHN MILTON
English poet

FOR MANY EXPLORERS the adventure is the goal; and after it is over, they are content to reflect privately on what they learned. Not all voyagers want to produce a book.

You may be satisfied to have explored your inner life by means of writing and feel no inclination to leave a written record. If you would like to assemble your chapters into a book, however, read the following pages for suggestions.

IF YOU HAVE NOT WRITTEN FINAL DRAFTS

You may have written numerous rough drafts that you haven't yet taken time to revise and write in final form. If this has happened, simply use your rough drafts for the book. The task of revising and writing final versions of many drafts is burdensome, a chore likely to be postponed and never done. It's much better to have an assembled book of first drafts.

Consider how we cherish the handwritten diaries of our ancestors. They are unrevised rough drafts. You have accomplished the important part, the writing itself. Now proceed to follow the directions on the following pages.

A few people who haven't written final drafts do rally a burst of energy, work within a specified length of time, and in a great flurry complete their final versions; however, of the people who intend to do this, most place their rough drafts in a drawer, never find the time, and evermore feel guilty.

Here is a solution. If you prefer a typed final draft but can't dispatch it yourself, hire a student or a neighbor who types, or a clever grandchild who has learned computer keyboarding, or hire a professional typist to do this task for you.

Of course, if you are writing for broad publication or for an academic class, then you will want to thoroughly and carefully revise and proofread all your writings. Refer to chapters 28 and 29, and assiduously apply those skills to each entry you've written.

ANOTHER CONSIDERATION

As you read through everything you've written, you may become aware that you avoided a difficult but important subject. This is not unusual. We often write around the most uncomfortable subjects, never about them. If this has happened to you, take time to imagine writing the words you've avoided. Quite possibly they should remain outside of your memoirs. Frequently, however, we find that the most difficult topics are filled with energy, depth, and power; in writing about them we discover still more spiritual dimensions in ourselves.

One way of handling this quandary is to go ahead and write about the avoided subject, but then put that chapter away for a while. Let several weeks go by before you look at it again, and then reread it in the context of your other chapters. At that time you'll probably have a sense of whether it should be included. Even if you decide to exclude this piece, you're likely to find that writing it was beneficial. To write about traumatic experiences is usually cleansing and can even lead to feelings of reconciliation. On the other hand, this piece may turn out to be the most dynamic and important part of your book.

The man who writes about himself and his own time
is the only man who writes about all people and about all time.
—GEORGE BERNARD SHAW
Irish playwright, critic, novelist

Ask yourself if you want readers of your memoirs to know something about you that you've not yet told. You've reread all your chapters and looked through your greenhouse file. Look at the heart you filled with important subjects and at your lists of topics. Consider whether you've neglected an aspect of yourself; if this is so, take time now to write about it.

WRITING TO ACCURATELY RE-CREATE REALITY

Even the most vividly written memoirs cannot replicate an actual event; some falsity is inherent because the best chosen words cannot duplicate the actual flames of experience. The writer can only mirror those flames, and in the process certain distortions occur. Although slight discrepancy is inevitable, the underlying truth of your inner life will be apparent.

> *The last thing that we find in making a book*
> *is to know what we must put first.*

—BLAISE PASCAL
French religious thinker, mathematician, physicist

THE PARTS OF YOUR BOOK

Title Page

You'll find a basic title page in figure 12. Copy it or design your own title page.

The Introduction

Write a brief introduction. Tell about your present circumstances, your age, and your involvements and interests. Describe your decision to undertake the writing of your memoirs.

Author Photograph

The page following your introduction is a good location for a photograph of yourself. Identify it with your full, legal name and also with any nicknames. Place a caption under the picture telling what was happening in your life when it was taken.

The Chapters

One way of deciding how to organize your chapters is to spread them out on a table so that you can see all the titles. Then lay them out with the edges overlapping like a large hand of cards. Arrange and rearrange them until their order feels right. They can be arranged chronologically, in the order in which you wrote them, or in the order in which you'd like them to be read. Trust your intuition.

Bret Lott's memoirs, *Fathers, Sons, and Brothers,* interweaves chapters about his own father and brothers with chapters about himself and his sons. When he was ready to arrange and sequence the chapters, Lott placed them on his living room floor and physically moved them about.

Number pages consecutively from beginning to end. Handwritten numbers are acceptable.

The Conclusion

Your retrospective chapter is likely to serve well as a conclusion. Writers occasionally like to add further thoughts or a favorite meditation or prayer.

The Date

Write the current date on the last page.

The Memoirs

of

_____
YOUR NAME

written in _____
YEAR

Figure 12

PRODUCTION OF YOUR BOOK

Call your favorite copy shop to find out if it carries acid-free paper. If it does not, buy the necessary quantity of acid-free paper from a stationery or art supply shop and take it with you to the copy shop.

An employee at the shop can adjust the machinery to make sharp copies of the photographs and documents you've placed in your manuscript. Faded exposures can be reproduced with increased contrast, resulting in copies clearer than the originals.

Buy binders for the manuscripts. Stores that sell notebooks are good places to shop. Look at the kinds of bindings that open and will allow you to add any chapters you may write in the future. If you want to have your book professionally bound, look in the yellow pages of your telephone directory under "Book binderies." Many printing shops also bind books. Another option is the inexpensive comb binding that can be opened, available at most copy shops.

SHARE AND CELEBRATE YOUR BOOK

With trepidation, trust, and love, give this personal gift to the people who are dear to you. Consider also placing copies in the libraries of organizations and religious institutions to which you belong. The sharing of your life will open dialogues with other people and bring about gratifying new understandings and relationships.

> *A good book is the purest essence of a human soul.*
> —SPEECH IN SUPPORT OF THE LONDON LIBRARY, 1840
> F. Harrison's *Carlyle and the London Library*

THE GREAT EXPEDITION

You have written earnestly and candidly about your inner life. You've shown your thoughts and feelings through periods of both difficulty and happiness. You've written about many of your dreams and struggles and the people and places most meaningful to you—and you may continue to write further chapters.

Your book shows your quest to find the meaning in your life. You may marvel at its ultimate mystery or—if your expedition has been graced—you may have glimpsed your cup of completeness, of communion. You have shown the routes you've traveled, the signs that guided you, the lamps that lit your way; and in rereading the story of your trek, you may realize yet new territories to explore.

THE GREATER FULFILLMENT

Though the book you have written is valuable as a gift to its readers, many writers have found that the experience of writing is even more fulfilling than the satisfaction of having produced a book. The writing itself may have been a spiritual experience. Yale

Professor Jaroslav Pelikan said about the writing of *The Consolation of Philosophy* by the medieval philosopher Boethius:

"The very act of writing, the kind of dredging up of these questions and these tentative answers out of the past and out of the inner self—that very process, putting it down, trying to say it right, is the consolation. And so it is in the work of writing the work that the consolation comes, as it is in the quest that the finding comes. For a spiritual quest means precisely that: not starting in a vacuum at square one, but starting where we are with what we have and with what we have found, to quest for it again. In Augustine's beautiful term, it is *fides quaerens intellectum*—faith in search of understanding—so that, having found understanding, faith can search yet again. Over and over."

This final excerpt, written by a workshop participant, is longer than previous selections, but it is included because it is exceptionally insightful, beautiful, and a testimony to the power of introspective writing. Because the writer must remain anonymous to protect the confidentiality of her patients, she cannot be credited. Please remember her story after you have completed this book, and be inspired by it to continue writing the memoirs of your soul.

After my daughter died, I could not think of what to do with myself. Nothing made sense, the past had been swallowed by darkness, I could not even remember anything about her except for the last few weeks when life slowly seeped out of her. I could not project into the future, could not illuminate any part of the horrid eternal absence of her to guide my next step. So I instinctively continued what I had been doing, put one step in front of another, went to work every morning, fixed dinner every night, blindly, woodenly.

Reality did not cooperate with my wish not to feel, not to notice. I am a psychiatrist and my patients brought emotions which were dynamite. They spoke of being depressed, of wanting to die, wishing to kill themselves. Some knew that my daughter had died of suicide after many years of depression and remissions. But what could they talk about if not what was inside them?

And I was changing. I worried that I could not provide what my patients needed; I could not think as clearly as usual, my memory failed me. I had to look up the name and dosage of medicines I had used for years. I double-checked every decision I made, every prescription I wrote, terrified of mistakes. I consulted with colleagues to insure that my clinical decisions were based on the status of the patients, not on what had just happened in my family. Many of my patients were suicidal—it is the bread and butter of a psychiatrist's work—and I had always known that I stood firmly on the side of life for them. But now such stance was threatened by the immense love for my daughter, my empathy for her choice, my desire to join her. I knew that I could not offer the usual safe mooring to my patients.

In turn, their stories, their struggles, their pull toward blackness felt like cruel enticements to me in my fragility. I referred several patients to colleagues and tried to persuade others to work with a different doctor. But they would not, they cried that I was abandoning them, and I did not have the heart, the courage to oppose them. For weeks the situation weighed me down, I could not find peace, could not sleep.

Finally my body gave up and thereby rescued me in some fashion. Respiratory infection spread, resistive to treatment, and I finally had to give up when I could not speak anymore. A fitting end.

There were three months of the preoccupation of physical illness. I was weak, unsure, distracted by pain, in wait for others to find out what to do, which antibiotics would finally work. It felt right to be passive, not to be offered alternatives which my mind would not have been able to consider.

When I could think again, I came to recognize the dark coldness of depression. It was, I saw, very different from grief. Grief was a tribute to my daughter, a measure of her importance, of her stature in my heart which was gorged with love as well as sorrow. It was an alive feeling, as much as I hated being alive. It was an imaginative, creative state, generous in giving me the sight of her face, the very texture of her skin in my fingertips, the weight of her body against my chest. I hated the absolute knowledge of her absence, and I loved the glowing knowledge of the life we had shared.

In contrast, depression was subtractive, focused on my failings or errors in the self-centeredness of guilt and shame, and my heart became a bitter stone, small and immeasurably dense. It felt as if I were standing, with leaden feet, in the silently rushing waters of the river Styx. My consciousness was distracted, and depression thus robbed me all over again of my daughter.

I fought it as I know how and it worked, little by little. Among other things, I decided to use classes; being a student has always been a pleasure for me. I had dreamt of retirement giving me time for art, and I enrolled in a class which brought back to me a welcomed awareness of color. The community college also offered adult creative writing classes. I thought I hated writing, I knew I was often late in completing paperwork, dreaded the dictation of long reports. Words were so weighty, the search so exacting to properly express and document findings, the consequences of incorrectness severe for patients and myself. But I have loved reading since childhood, have a great debt of gratitude to authors for the pleasure, guidance, and companionship they offered me. One class was titled Women's Writing, a review of literature and creative writing combined, and that sold me on it.

The teacher had a lopsided charm, she was easygoing, enthusiastic about literature, lightly cynical about life. She chose lovely gems for us to read by United States and Canadian authors of the last 150 years. The group of students was generous in spirit, with an appetite for experience and the trust to share it, which lifted us above self-consciousness.

And the words came to me, unexpected gifts borne without struggle. They gave form to what I felt. For the first time I knew firsthand the alchemy of art, the passage from experience to expression which transforms pain into beauty, pleasure. What we wrote was not important stuff, yet profoundly meaningful. We played well together, appreciating spontaneity. I ranted, cried on paper, and came out loving the whole thing. My classmates liked to hear my words and I listened to, tasted theirs with admiration and gratitude. I wrote about now and way back when, sensing again the vivid course of life, no longer the frozen sludge of depression.

To stop practicing medicine had meant so many losses, of which I became aware in stages. Professional identity had been a big part of my self-concept for forty years. It had stood for goodness, dedication, intelligence, and I felt diminished without it. I missed the trusting exchange with patients, the warm connection with colleagues. I missed being a worker, rushing out of my office for a quick lunch downtown with all the other people who make things run. I replaced some of that by catching up on women friends, joining groups.

Only after I began to write, though, did I become aware of something precious I thought I had lost and missed intensely. As a psychotherapist, a unique part of my brain, psyche, spirit was engaged in a rich journey of discovery, using the patient's and my emotions as well as words. We communicated empathetically, intellectually, verbally, and it was my job to let the information collect inside me, feel it, taste it, weigh it, and to convey my sense of its meaning to the person across from me, using words familiar and cogent. After a few months of writing, as I sat with emotions, images, sensations, recollections, waiting for the words to come up that would describe them, I recognized that the same process was at work. I remember being washed over by a wave of gratitude, with surprise and joy. I was given back, in a new package, the gift of myself. With a casual toss of beneficence, life had even added new ways to manifest the gift of being.

CHAPTER 28

Revising to Energize Your Writing

To revise is to

$\longrightarrow$ PUT IN

$\longleftarrow$ TAKE OUT

transform and

FLIP ABOUT

WE DON'T REVISE as we write the original draft because to do so would interrupt the voyage. It would slow us down, causing us to lose sight of what's ahead. We would miss the upcoming turn; we might not even get to the upcoming turn. Instead of steering by the stars, we would be stumbling over rocks. Travel with the meteoric rush of words in your first draft, knowing you can edit them later.

Revision is optional for those who are writing for themselves and a few close friends. The majority of writers find that their quick rough drafts are much improved when revised, but some writers don't like to revise, and others are satisfied with rough drafts.

If your memoirs might be seen by people in your community and saved by your descendants, you will probably want to express yourself as effectively as possible. Look upon revision as an opportunity to strengthen and enrich your writing. Revision, unlike proofreading, can be marvelously creative.

If you are writing your memoirs for broad publication or as part of an academic course, then you will find revision essential for the production of high-quality work. In fact, you may want to ask your response group not only to point out strengths in your writing and pose questions but also to report their personal responses to your writing and make suggestions. Every time you meet, bring a copy of your rough draft for each member of your response group so that as you read aloud everyone can follow visually and write comments on your draft. Ask your listeners to return their annotated copies to you so you can carefully consider all their remarks before making your revisions.

The ideal time to revise your writing is after you've heard it read aloud and after you've answered the questions suggested for reflection. Revision should be completed before you proofread for mechanical correctness, including spelling, punctuation, capitalization, paragraphing, grammar, and correct word usage. To revise your rough draft, you'll add, delete, change, and rearrange. Postpone proofreading until just before you write the final draft.

Most professional writers spend far more time revising than they do writing first drafts. Paul Valéry, an esteemed French writer renowned for his style, said that great writers never finish revising their work; eventually they must abandon it.

ADD TO YOUR ROUGH DRAFT

Provide Necessary Supplementary Information

You'll first want to add information. Your oral reading and listeners' questions have revealed what needs to be clarified. When we hear listeners' responses to readings, we often realize we've inadvertently left out essential information. A middle-aged writer recounted an incident that had happened when she was sixteen, but she failed to mention that she had been a teenager at the time. When she saw the effect her story had on listeners, she realized at once that she needed to add information about her age. Note listeners' questions in your margins so that later you'll remember what further information may be needed.

If you do add information, make use of the alternating blank lines. You may also write supplementary paragraphs to insert in the appropriate places. Expand your draft as much as necessary to make each chapter complete.

Add Sensory Data

When working on your rough draft, you wrote rapidly and impulsively. You followed your story wherever it led. You made a quick sketch. Now you're ready to introduce sensory description.

The most evocative sense is smell, but writers who don't know this frequently forget to include it. Realtors know the importance of smell. Some realtors arrive at a house before it is shown to bake cookie dough in the oven so that when prospective buyers walk in the door they'll feel the house is homey and inviting.

Smell and taste can be more challenging to convey with words than the other senses; sometimes you'll need to make comparisons. For example, the smell of a kitchen where milk spilled and soured could be compared to the smell of a sauerkraut factory.

All things and living creatures, as well as places, have some sort of odor. We think of smell when we see flowers, but weeds smell, too. Earth has a smell. Animals and people smell. In describing her grandmother, Adrienne Lannom wrote:

> *Grandma had a special smell that was unlike any other.... I think it was a combination of baking and cooking smells, especially bread-making smells, and the smell of a lotion she ritually applied every night after she unpinned and brushed her hair.*

The sense of touch refers to not only the textures and temperatures we feel against our skin. It also includes:

- Body awareness or kinesthetic feeling
    - ~ Tension in muscles
    - ~ Changes in respiration
    - ~ Sensations in the stomach, throat, and elsewhere
    - ~ Awareness of clothing
- Atmosphere
    - ~ Movement or density of the air
    - ~ Temperature and humidity

When you describe sounds, remember to include background noises as well as nearby sounds. Also, analyze the sounds you make with your own body. For example, if you are now sitting at a computer, notice that while the machine hums you may occasionally creak your chair, and you might sniff or clear your throat. Someone may speak to you, and you may answer. Workers beyond your window might clatter trash cans while a garbage truck whines as it compresses its load. As an exercise, analyze all the perceptible sounds you hear now; later, when you recall the event of your narrative, remember or reconstruct the many sounds at that scene.

Sight is the most described sense. You've probably shown how the setting, people, and objects looked, but you may not have described the lighting. To add depth and atmosphere to your description, tell what kind of light was present, its angle and its brightness. Mention shadows or dark places.

Taste is less frequently important in our experiences, but its inclusion flavors our writing. If your first kiss was minty because your date chewed spearmint gum, share this sensation with the reader.

Of course, you would not want to include all your senses in all your descriptions, but be aware that some sensory description will enrich your writing. To select which senses are appropriate for a particular chapter, think back on the experience, identify the predominant sensations, and feature them.

Include Quotations

If you can remember, even approximately, what you said and what other people said, insert quotes. Quotations add individuality and animation.

Disclose Your Feelings

Sometimes writers tell what events occurred but neglect to reveal the emotions they felt. To show your feelings in indirect ways is fine and is often preferable to stating them. Either show them indirectly or state what you felt, but don't leave readers unaware of how you reacted to the important experiences in your life.

Indicate the Significance of the Experience

Often the significance of an experience is evident to ourselves in the context of our lives; however, readers may not understand why the event was important. Try the "So what?" test. Say to yourself, "This experience happened to me, so what? What is its meaning for me? What difference did it make in my life?" Then examine what you wrote to see if the reader will understand why you chose to write about this happening and how it made a difference.

MAKE DELETIONS

Cross out. Scribble over. Eliminate ineffective writing with a few quick strokes. Reconsider trite thought patterns and eradicate clichés. Your creative well will not run dry; rather, you'll dig deeper to fresher water.

MAKE CHANGES

Replace Vapid Verbs with Vigorous Verbs

Verbs are a writer's most powerful medium. Choose the most vivid, descriptive verbs available. The following exercise was devised by a talented teacher, Sister Helena Brand, SNJM, who taught at Marylhurst College. As you read the scene, say an expressive verb when you come to the blanks.

He _____ down the hall.

She _____ on the couch.

"Is that you, Frank?" she _____.

"Yes," he _____ as he _____ her.

If you chose pale, vague verbs, your scene will be bland, like this one:

He walked down the hall.
She lay on the couch.
"Is that you, Frank?" she asked.
"Yes," he said as he saw her.

If you chose vital, vigorous verbs, however, your scene will convey more drama and be more engaging.

He swaggered down the hall.
She trembled on the couch.
"Is that you, Frank?" she whispered.
"Yes," he sneered as he grabbed her.
Or:
He tiptoed down the hall.
She crouched on the couch.
"Is that you, Frank?" she hissed.
"Yes," he gulped as he shrank from her.

Experiment with many different verbs, and revise this scene in a variety of ways. Then read the rough draft of any chapter in your memoirs, underlining its verbs. Consider replacing the general, vague verbs with vital verbs whenever such a change would be appropriate.

Replace General Nouns with Specific Nouns

When you see that you've used a general noun, replace it with a specific one. Instead of saying someone had a dog, tell us he had a Labrador retriever. Better yet, give us a picture of a gaunt, stiff Labrador retriever with a gray muzzle or a playful, sleek black Lab. Generic nouns give us only fuzzy, colorless pictures, while concrete nouns convey clear, specific images.

Here are examples of general nouns and specific nouns:

General	*Specific*
Tree	Tulip tree with waxy leaves
Cake	German chocolate cake
Song	"You Are My Sunshine"
Coat	Wrinkled, khaki trench coat
Pen	Blue Paper Mate ballpoint pen

Change the Passive Voice to the Active Voice

The active voice feels more alive and immediate than the passive voice. Its pattern is: subject, verb, object. Here is an example: Roberto pitched the ball.

The passive voice is less dynamic. Its pattern is object, verb, subject. For example: The ball was pitched by Roberto. This voice is flaccid. Can you imagine a sports announcer speaking this way? We would not feel the pulse of the game.

Rewrite the following sentences, changing them from passive to active voice. Examples:

> A rousing song was sung by Frogel.
> Frogel bellowed a bawdy ditty.
> The marathon was won by Zoster.
> Zoster burst through the finish line ribbon.

Your turn (remember to choose a vivid verb):

> The chocolate mousse was eaten by Clovis.
> A stern lecture was given by the matron.
> A gazelle was eaten by a pride of lions.

The passive voice is evasive. When the subject is not named, the "doer" escapes responsibility: a mistake was made, action will be taken. Office memos sometimes take this form. The passive voice is useful when the writer wants to be vague. For most writing, and for writing memoirs, however, we want the energy, directness, and responsibility of the active voice. Compare "I hugged her" with "She was hugged by me."

Some writers habitually use the passive voice without being aware that they employ this sentence structure. Since use of the passive voice is not usually a conscious, narrative choice, careful writers often ask listeners to inform them whenever they hear the passive voice. Ask the listeners in your response group to do this for you.

Replace Verbs of "Being"

Replace "It is," "There is," "There were," "There was," with specific subjects and vigorous verbs. For example, instead of writing "It was raining," a bland sentence, you could write "Rain pelted us" or "Rain misted into our hair and sweaters."

Here are more examples:

> There was a dog inside the fence.

Drop "There was," replace "dog" with a specific noun, and choose a vital verb.

> A snarling Akita paced inside the fence.

Here are more changed sentences:

There were lots of ants.
Countless ants milled over the potato salad and fried chicken.
It was a dusty room.
Cobwebs hung from lampshades, and dust dulled the tabletops.

For practice, change the following sentences. Drop "It was" and "There was." Begin each sentence with a precise noun followed by a vigorous verb.

It was a windy day.
It was hard for the old man to see the sign.
There was a child in a high chair.
There was a clock in the hall.
There was a mosquito in our tent.

When you are writing a first draft, ignore all these editing considerations. Be oblivious to verb and noun choices, voice, and "being" constructions. As you write, be conscious only of the experience you're remembering. Worrying about stylistic considerations as you venture into realms of reminiscence would distract you and impede your fluency. In skipping lines, you're leaving room to revise later. Step four of the writing process is the effective time to underline your verbs, replace vapid verbs with vital ones, replace generic nouns, change sentences from the passive to the active voice, and rewrite sentences that start with "being" constructions.

Rearrange Sections of Writing
You may realize that certain paragraphs or sentences should have preceded others. Fine! Circle what you want to move, and draw arrows. Change the sequence of big or small sections in your chapters.

THE REVISED, EDITED DRAFT
The foregoing suggestions are basic and serviceable and are used to good effect by memoirists, but they are not the only techniques writers use. Be aware that some writers scrutinize their sentences for word repetition, check to see that sentence length and structure is varied, listen for pleasing cadences, and apply other editing subtleties. You will automatically employ many of these sophisticated techniques when you make changes as a result of hearing your draft read aloud. If you wish to understand further strategies for revision and editing, see the books by William Strunk Jr. and E. B. White and by William Zinsser listed under Suggested Reading and References on page 253.

A thoroughly revised draft may be marked so much and contain so many insertions that it is difficult to read. Such reworking is typical of the majority of professional writers. Literary scholars enjoy studying the sequence of drafts by famous writers to observe how their poems or prose evolved. People who do not aspire to write literary art, however, do not need to revise their drafts many times. Engaging memoirs can be achieved by simply taking time to add, delete, change, and rearrange.

The beautiful part of writing is that
you don't have to get it right the first time,
unlike, say, a brain surgeon.
You can always do it better, find the exact word,
the apt phrase, the leaping simile.

—ROBERT CORMIER
American author, columnist, and reporter

CHAPTER 29

Proofreading for Polished Prose

Proofread carefully to see if you any words out.

—AUTHOR UNKNOWN

SOME WRITERS WANT their rough drafts to be proofread by an expert who holds a red pen. Such serious proofreading is not usually necessary unless you plan to have your memoirs published for broad distribution or you are a student writing for academic credit. If your memoirs are written for your family and close friends, you can achieve a satisfactory level of standard English by first checking the big units—the paragraphs—then the sentences, and finally, individual words.

PARAGRAPHS

Glance at the pages of your rough draft. If you find only one paragraph on a page, you've probably run paragraphs together. See where your text shifts from one idea to a different one—where, if you were reading aloud you would take a breath and might change your tone of voice. Mark those places for paragraph breaks.

If you quoted speakers, check also to see that you began a new paragraph each time you changed speakers. This is a visual clue to readers. Changing to a new paragraph is like turning one's head from one speaker to another; it helps readers know that a different person is talking.

SENTENCES
Run-Ons

Many people make the error of writing "run-ons," sentences that run together. An effective way to catch them is to read your draft aloud, sentence by sentence, *from the end of your chapter to the beginning, listening to each separate sentence.* Reading your chapter in reverse order lifts sentences out of their context and allows you to hear them individually. By listening to each sentence as it is spoken, you'll hear the merged sentences. This method of catching run-ons sounds bizarre, and the first time you try it you may feel strange, but eventually you'll appreciate its efficacy.

In a quiet, private place where you won't feel self-conscious, read the last sentence of your chapter aloud. You'll know if it's a single sentence by listening to it. If it is two or more sentences, separate them. Then read the next-to-the-last sentence and listen to it. From the end of your chapter to the beginning, proceed to read and listen to each sentence, and separate those that run together.

Fragments

What if one of the sentences you read sounded incomplete? It could be a fragment that needs a subject or a verb. Consider whether it's effective alone. Fragments may be used to good effect, but accidental fragments can weaken your writing. Imagine a stranger walking up to you and saying only the partial sentence you wrote. Would you nod or feel bewildered? Listen to the sentence again to decide if the fragment is all right as it is or if you should make it into a full sentence by adding the missing part.

Displeasing Constructions

Persuade a good friend to read your draft aloud to you. You'll hear overused words, awkward phrasings, and confusing constructions. These problems are more apparent when someone else reads your draft aloud to you than when you read it. Once you've identified what doesn't sound right, you can change your sentences until they make sense and do sound satisfactory.

WORDS
Spelling and Homonyms

Spelling can be checked by your computer using the spellchecker function or a proofreader. If you must find your own misspellings, give your draft a cursory reading only for spelling, circle the words in question, and look up all of them in one spelling session.

Remember, however, that if you are using the spellchecker function on your computer, it will not catch spellings that may change the meaning and intent of your draft. It does not, for example, distinguish between misused homonyms such as "here" and "hear" or "there" and "their"—words that sound alike but have different meanings.

One of the most commonly misused homonyms is *its/it's*. Actually, this usage is simple to master if you remember that any time you use *it's* you must be able to substitute *it is*. *It's* means *it is*. The apostrophe shows where the letter *i* was dropped. *It's* is the contraction of two words. Many people mistakenly think they should use the form with the apostrophe to show possession; however, because the contracted form has the apostrophe, *its* without an apostrophe indicates ownership. For example: It's *(it is)* a fine day! The kitten drank its (we cannot substitute *it is*) dish of milk. Use *it's* only when you can substitute *it is*; use *its* the rest of the time.

Some other homonyms to be aware of are *affect/effect, alter/altar, capitol/capital, weather/whether, course/coarse, whose/who's, council/counsel, dye/die, sense/since, past/passed, loose/lose, through/threw, wear/where,* and *break/brake.* These are only some of the many troublesome homonyms that complicate a writer's work. Most grammar books and writers manuals include lists of homonyms and give their definitions.

Nominative and Objective Cases

Another common error is the use of pronouns in the nominative case after prepositions, a mistake that jars the ears of most educated listeners and readers. Examples of this misuse are: "The invitation was addressed to Jennifer and I." "The horse was given to Carol and he." "Please make a reservation for my wife and I."

This mistake occurs most often when the pronoun is linked with a preceding name. If the other name is dropped, the writer can usually hear the mistake. She would not say, "The invitation was addressed to I," or "The horse was given to he," or "Please make a reservation for I." If you are unclear about when to use pronouns in the nominative case and when to use them in the objective case, refer to a handbook for writers or a grammar book.

Transitive and Intransitive Verbs

Correct use of *lie* and *lay* bewilders many people. If you're writing for your family and friends, proceed to write the way you speak, but if you are writing for a broader readership, refer to your handbook. *Lie* and *lay* are especially tricky because their transitive and intransitive forms shift through the past, present, and future tenses. You'll find a reference chart helpful.

Sit and *set* and *rise* and *raise* are misused almost as often as *lie* and *lay*. Review the rules about their use in your handbook.

These various proofreading suggestions address some of the most common mistakes. You can catch most of them yourself, but if you do plan to publish your memoirs and don't feel well-informed about word choices, ask more than one person to proofread for you before you write the final draft. Most community colleges provide a writing lab where advanced students assist other students who bring their drafts in for inspection, so you might talk with the lab director about hiring one of the advanced students to proofread your memoirs if you want to be sure your final draft conforms to the conventions of standard English.

I was working on the proof of one of my poems
all the morning and took out a comma.
In the afternoon I put it back again.

—OSCAR WILDE
Irish playwright, poet, and short story writer

Suggestions for Academic Instructors, Workshop Facilitators, and Writing Partners

We have an opportunity to revision education as a communal enterprise from the foundations up—in our images of reality, in our modes of knowing, in our ways of teaching and learning.... Such a re-visioning would result in a deeply ethical education, an education that would help students develop the capacity for connectedness that is at the heart of an ethical life. In such an education, intellect and spirit would be one, teachers and learners and subjects would be in vital community with one another, and a world in need of healing would be well served.

—Parker J. Palmer
Educational reformer and writer

MEMOIRS OF THE SOUL is a textbook, a workshop resource, and a guide for partners writing together. Its chapters originated in handouts I prepared for the workshops I lead, so they have been thoroughly tested. While ideas for people who are writing together are scattered throughout the book, this chapter offers more detailed suggestions for academic and other group settings.

THE MEMOIR: A LITERARY GENRE

If you follow the chapters as they are sequenced in this book, the first ones will delineate characters and place and reveal the main character's goals and problems. These chapters are followed by rising action and complications that lead to one or more crises. Dramatic tension mounts until it reaches a climax when we see what the outcome will be; after that, a resolution, or dénouement, reveals how the main character comes to terms with all that has happened. Thus, in a loose, general way the chapters of this book will help shape the writers' memoirs according to classical literary form (see figure 13 for more details).

At the back of the book you will find lists of suggested writers' guides, memoirs and autobiographies, anthologies, and books of particular interest to instructors and workshop leaders. You and the writers in your group can extend these lists.

ACADEMIC INSTRUCTION

Ask students to write reviews of the published memoirs and autobiographies they read and to make copies of their reviews for all members of the class. Everyone will thus have a guide from which to choose books. Collections of reviews from past classes can comprise a small library for use by current students.

Consider requiring your students to keep diologic journals of their readings. To keep a diologic journal, the reader folds a page of lined paper vertically. To the left of the fold, the reader copies any phrase or sentence from the book that elicits his reaction, whether of agreement, disagreement, surprise, or any other emotion. To the right of the fold, the reader writes to the author or to one of the characters in the book. The reader may argue, advise, congratulate, or engage in any other form of dialogue. The vertically folded paper is used for a bookmark so the reader can conveniently add to it while reading the book. If the reader rages or philosophizes in response to the author, the journal can grow to numerous pages in length. The keeping of a diologic journal engages the reader and is useful later when writing a book review. Grade the journal according to the amount of understanding and involvement with the book it shows, not by whether the reader agrees or disagrees with the perspective of the author.

Particular Admonitions

You must not assess the content of your students' writing! Because their writing will be profoundly personal, you must evaluate it indirectly. Memoirs by their nature are candid. To elicit skillfully written, candid memoirs you must assess only:

- The students' adherence to the steps of the writing process
- Participation in response groups
- Mastery of writing skills

DELINEATION OF CHARACTERS AND CIRCUMSTANCES —

Subjects for Your Memoirs
Breathing Life into Your Writing
Internalized Places
The Soul of a Child
People Who Etched an Imprint
Adolescent Angst

RISING ACTIONS —

Events That Shaped the Course of Your Life
Evolving Ideas about Religion
Struggles and Satisfactions
Focusing on Your Subject
Transitions
Joinings and Separations
Chance and Choice
Aspirations

CLIMAXES AND REVELATIONS —

Confronting Crisis
Longings
Love
Flip of the Compass
Inner Peace
Dreams and Visions
Encountering the Numinous
Spiritual Well-Being
Gratitude

DÉNOUEMENT —

A Retrospective Overview and Insights
The Gift of Yourself

Figure 13

Several chapters in this book should be optional, if used at all, in credit courses. They are chapters 17, 19, 22, 23, and 24. Some workshop participants who have used this book found that they were not ready to confront the major crises in their lives. They said they might return to chapter 17 later, when they feel emotionally ready to look at traumas they are not yet able to face. Working with chapter 19 could be uncomfortably revealing and personal for some students, while chapters 22 and 23 open subjects students may feel strange disclosing in a credit course. Chapter 24 requires experience and perspective younger students may not yet have. All of these chapters are valuable for individuals who write their spiritual memoirs but may be inappropriate, and certainly should be optional, in graded classes.

Require all students to take part in response groups for the assigned chapters, but allow students to indicate which final drafts they want to submit for grades. Not every topic will work equally well for every writer, and not every final draft has to be graded.

Imperative Advice

Memoirs of the Soul is a prescriptive book only in terms of method. It should never be used for doctrinaire purposes. Because it invites disclosure, a well-meaning teacher could do great damage if she were to try to "correct" the feelings and thoughts of the writer. Teachers as well as students must follow the guidelines for listeners. A sensitive teacher might pose a question that would guide the writer toward self-examination, but any judgmental response would violate the trust and the integrity of the writer.

Assessment for Academic Credit

Grades can be based on:

- Completion of a designated percentage of writing assignments
- Incorporation of the steps of the writing process
- Unfailing participation in response groups
- Conformity of final drafts to the conventions of standard English and the elements of style taught by the instructor
- Thoughtful diologic reading journals
- Analytical book reviews

If you ask students to use these six criteria to grade themselves, they will reflect on their effort as well as their achievement. Most students grade themselves more severely than we would grade them, and you will have the pleasure of raising some of their grades.

The basis for grades should be printed in the course description and syllabus. In addition, make it clear that you will not judge the content of your students' memoirs and will guard the confidentiality of every student's writing.

For further information about teaching memoir-writing at university and secondary levels, please read my article about how to evoke and sensitively assess writing that probes values and seeks ultimate meanings, "A Reflection on Classroom Teaching." It is posted on www.memoirworkshops.com under "Academic Considerations."

INSIGHTS FOR ALL INSTRUCTORS AND WORKSHOP FACILITATORS

Since the writing of Saint Augustine's *Confessions*, the confession has been a component of memoirs. Whenever we reflect on our inner lives, we confront the acts we have suffered and the deeds we have committed. Confession is inevitable. You must create a safe environment so participants can explore their deepest regrets as well as their great joys. Do not reveal that you are shocked. Though you will be confronted with surprising confidences, you must remain accepting and empathic.

Sometimes writers will bring narratives for you alone to read. Those writers aren't ready to share what they have written with response groups, and their writing may reveal suffering that will distress you. When the next class or workshop meets, find time to speak quietly and privately to such a writer. Thank her for placing trust in you and commend her for being able to write about the problem. Then, if appropriate, ask the writer if she has found a good counselor. Most writers will say that they have, but if someone has not found a helpful counselor, be prepared to suggest resources. Have ready appropriate telephone numbers for mental health services, rape crisis counselors, or other suitable hotlines. Do not attempt to counsel the writer yourself unless you are a professionally trained, licensed, and insured counselor.

To write about what we have suffered, both as victims and inflictors, is cleansing and healing. Writing expels the experience from deep within oneself and allows one to dissociate from it and examine it. Through such writing we are sometimes able to forgive, to find forgiveness, and to regain self-respect. You are honored with trust when a student makes you part of this process.

Always write rough drafts along with students and participants. To expect them to disclose their inner lives while withholding your own personal life does not create a participatory atmosphere. You may choose not to reveal yourself as fully as you would if you were writing among peers; nevertheless, you should participate in both the writing and responding in order to promote comfort and enthusiasm in the students. The response groups provide an opportunity to build collegiality.

When you take part in response groups, do not assume the role of facilitator. Participants, even younger students, should be the ones to decide who will read first and when to move on to the next reader. By following the guidelines for listening and responding, students and participants are perfectly able to manage the response groups themselves, and they gain control of the process by doing so.

Prior to opening certain chapters, alert participants to make special preparations:

- Chapter 12—Bring a snapshot picturing a person, place, or object important to the writer.
- Chapter 18—Bring something that is meaningful to the writer such as a prayer, poem, work of art, selection of music, handmade item, passage from literature, saved letter, or cherished gift.
- Chapter 24—Bring pencils or pens in at least five different colors for drawing lines.
- Chapter 26—Reread everything that's been written.

Credit Classes at the Secondary Level

Some chapters of this book are not appropriate for use with secondary students because they tend to be less compassionate as peer editors than adults. Because adolescents are not yet sure of and comfortable with their own identities, they are more likely to discuss classmates' disclosures. Immature students are likely to tell their friends what was revealed.

Even so, you can use *Memoirs of the Soul* as a high school textbook. Begin the course by first discussing the steps of the writing process and then the problem of confidentiality. Reassure students that you will not call their parents or talk about the students' writings in the teachers' lounge. Similarly, obtain an agreement of confidentiality from the class. If the students themselves discuss the potential for harm from peer gossip and then design their own confidentiality code, they are more likely to observe it. Encourage them to create a formal pledge of confidentiality that every class member would sign.

Another issue that could arise is the requirement placed on teachers to report indications of child abuse or intention to do harm. Therefore, explain to your students at the beginning of the course that you are required to inform counselors of abuse or dangerous situations. Writing is a powerful tool for healing, and most students benefit from writing about painful parts of their lives, but they should be aware that a counselor might have to be alerted.

Teamwork enables common people to attain uncommon results.
—BASED ON AN OBSERVATION BY ANDREW CARNEGIE
Business magnate and philanthropist

WORKSHOPS

Writers' organizations, lifelong learners, members of religious congregations, support groups, and people who seek to examine and understand their lives have found this book easy to use. Simply follow the boxed instructions.

Each chapter fits a two-hour session. To maintain group cohesion and momentum, plan to meet every week. Participants in full-time, intensive summer workshops can meet daily and complete a chapter a day. The chapters that follow chapter 3 initiate two writings, so if participants meet mornings and afternoons they will have time to take the warm-up writing through all the steps of the writing process during the morning and do the same with the second topic in the afternoon.

To organize a workshop, you'll first need to find a location. The pastoral care department of a hospital sponsored the class I conducted in preparation for this book and arranged for two different workshops to meet in hospital conference rooms on Saturday mornings and Sunday afternoons. In some communities, public utility companies allow local groups to use their meeting rooms, and a few banks make their conference rooms available on Saturdays. Bookstores frequently agree to remain open on certain evenings for literary groups. You may be able to use a room belonging to a religious organization, senior center, lifelong learning school, writers' group, or even the place where you work. People who don't drive or don't own cars will appreciate a location near public transportation.

Attract people to your workshop by sending announcements to newspapers, literary organizations, and publications for retired people. You may also wish to include newsletters written for religious groups and the organizations to which you belong, as well as the in-house letter of the business providing your meeting place. Be aware that newsletter editors often need to receive stories a month before publication time. Enclose page-size posters for bulletin boards along with your newsletter announcements. You may also be permitted to staple posters on bulletin boards in recreation centers, bookstores, shops, libraries, and places of worship.

Limit enrollment to twenty people. If more people wish to enroll, make a waiting list or schedule an additional section. Participants usually prefer to commit to only eight sessions at a time, with assurances that they may re-enroll for continuing sessions.

Plan to hold special, celebratory sessions after every eight chapters are completed, beginning with chapter 3. On these occasions invite participants to read selections from their writing to the group at large. Ahead of time announce that readings will be limited to a certain number of minutes so no one will monopolize the event, and ask a participant to time the readings. Continue to enforce the guidelines for good listening. Some writers may prefer to listen only, but the majority will want to read. Such events are a highlight of the workshop.

Critical to a successful workshop is the creation of a safe atmosphere. The workshop facilitator must ensure that listeners refrain from judging the behavior, lifestyles, and feelings expressed by the writers, and that members of the workshop guard the confidentiality of every writer. Discuss the guidelines for good listening the first time you meet, and remind participants of them at the next several sessions.

WRITING PARTNERS

A writing partner can be helpful in several ways. An ongoing, scheduled appointment with a partner will help sustain your writing momentum. If, before beginning to write, you talk to your partner about subjects you're considering, you'll automatically organize your ideas and find the right words. Once you've written a rough draft, your partner's responses will help you see its strengths and also recognize inadvertent omissions or ways it can be misconstrued. A good partnership energizes each writer and results in improved writing.

Use the guidelines throughout this book to respond to each other's drafts. These guidelines are designed to elicit constructive suggestions, protect your confidentiality, and shield you from personal criticism.

To find a writing partner:

- Let your friends and acquaintances know you're looking for a fellow writer.
- When you're among associates, announce that you're looking for a writing partner.
- If your community has a literary guild or community center where writing is taught, call to ask how critiquing groups are formed.
- Consider posting a "want ad" in a building where religious services are held.

Family members are not always ideal writing partners. Relatives tend to "correct" one's memories, to be judgmental, and to be less tactful than people from outside. If a relative wants to write with you, however, and is willing to follow the listening guidelines, you're likely to form a close familial bond in addition to writing your spiritual memoirs.

Couples who write together will see facets of their partners they might otherwise never glimpse. The resulting insights can lead to deeper understanding, increased appreciation, and greater spiritual intimacy.

> *Let us be united;*
> *Let us speak in harmony;*
> *Let our minds apprehend alike.*
> *Common be our prayer;*
> *Common be the end of our assembly;*
> *Common be our resolution;*
> *Common be our deliberations.*
> *Alike be our feelings;*
> *Unified be our hearts;*
> *Common be our intentions;*
> *Perfect be our unity.*

—THE RIG VEDA
Ancient Hindu hymns of praise

SUGGESTED READING AND REFERENCES

Writing Skills Books

The Elements of Style, William Strunk Jr. and E. B. White

On Writing Well: The Classic Guide to Writing Nonfiction, William K. Zinsser

Writing with Power: Techniques for Mastering the Writing Process, Peter Elbow

Memoirists' Guides

The Artist's Way: A Spiritual Path to Creativity, Julia Cameron

Going on Faith: Writing as a Spiritual Quest (formerly *Spiritual Quests: The Art and Craft of Religious Writing*), edited by William Zinsser

Inventing the Truth: The Art and Craft of Memoir, edited by William Zinsser

The Story of Your Life: Writing a Spiritual Autobiography, Dan Wakefield

Telling Your Story, Sam Keen

Writing as a Way of Healing: How Telling Our Stories Transforms Our Lives, Louise DeSalvo

Writing the Natural Way, Gabriele Rico

Memoirs and Autobiographies

The books on this list represent a variety of perspectives and cultures. The list is deliberately eclectic, and the books are not annotated because part of the adventure involves rummaging in libraries, picking up unfamiliar books, skimming them, and deciding whether to venture into the lives they open or to return them to the shelves. If an enticing title is not housed in your library, ask the reference librarian to order it for you through an interlibrary loan.

May you discover new realms of thought and feeling that will expand your understanding and the dimensions of your own spirituality.

About This Life: Journeys on the Threshold of Memory, Barry Lopez

All But My Life, Gerda Weissmann Klein

Alone Together, Elena Bonner

An American Childhood, Annie Dillard

And No Birds Sang, Farley Mowat

Apologia pro Vita Sua, Cardinal John Henry Newman

Apprentice to the Dawn: A Spiritual Memoir, James C. Ingebretsen

Autobiography of a Yogi, Paramahansa Yogananda

The Autobiography of Eleanor Roosevelt, Eleanor Roosevelt

The Autobiography of Malcolm X, Alex Haley

The Barn at the End of the World: The Apprenticeship of a Quaker, Buddhist Shepherd, Mary Rose O'Reilley

Black Elk Speaks, John G. Neihardt

Blessings in Disguise, Alec Guinness

Blowing Zen: Finding an Authentic Life, Ray Brooks

Called to Question: A Spiritual Memoir, Joan Chittister

Cave in the Snow: Tenzin Palmo's Quest for Enlightenment, Vicki Mackenzie

Children of the Manse, Lewis Richard Luchs

The Cloister Walk, Kathleen Norris

The Close: A Young Woman's First Year at Seminary, Chloe Breyer

The Color of Water: A Black Man's Tribute to His White Mother, James McBride

Confessions, Jean Jacques Rousseau

Confessions of St. Augustine, Aurelius Augustinus

The Consolation of Philosophy, Boethius

Dakota: A Spiritual Memoir, Kathleen Norris

The Dance of the Dissident Daughter: A Woman's Journey from Christian Tradition to the Sacred Feminine, Sue Monk Kidd

The Dark Child: The Autobiography of an African Boy, Camara Laye

Days of Obligation: An Argument with My Mexican Father, Richard Rodriguez

Death Be Not Proud, John Gunther

The Delights of Growing Old, Maurice Goudeket

Deliverance from Error, Abu Hamid al-Ghazali

Diary of a Zen Nun, Nan Shin

The Diary of Helena Morley, translated and edited by Elizabeth Bishop

Dust Tracks on a Road: An Autobiography, Zora Neale Hurston

Early Morning: Remembering My Father, William Stafford, Kim Robert Stafford

Fathering Words: The Making of an African American Writer, E. Ethelbert Miller

Fathers, Sons, & Brothers: The Men in My Family, Bret Lott

The Fruitful Darkness, Joan Halifax

Gray Is the Color of Hope, Irina Ratushinskaya

Growing Up, Russell Baker

Hope Against Hope: A Memoir, Nadezhda Mandelstam

I Know Why the Caged Bird Sings, Maya Angelou

The Imitation of Christ, Thomas à Kempis

In My Own Way: An Autobiography, Alan Watts

In Search of Sugihara: The Elusive Japanese Dipomat Who Risked His Life to Rescue 10,000 Jews from the Holocaust, Hillel Levine

Iron and Silk, Mark Salzman

Journal of a Solitude, May Sarton

Journey into the Whirlwind, Eugenia Semyonovna Ginzburg

Leaves from the Notebook of a Tamed Cynic, Reinhold Niebuhr

A Leg to Stand On, Oliver Sacks

Life in a Day, Doris Grumbach

Life in a Jewish Family, Edith Stein

A Life in School: What the Teacher Learned, Jane P. Tompkins

Living Faith, Jimmy Carter

Long Quiet Highway: Waking Up in America, Natalie Goldberg

A Long Way from Tipperary: What a Former Monk Discovered in his Search for the Truth,
     John Dominic Crossan

Looking for Mary (Or, the Blessed Mother and Me), Beverly Donofrio

Lost in Place: Growing up Absurd in Suburbia, Mark Salzman

The Magic Lantern: An Autobiogaphy, Ingmar Bergman

Meditations from a Movable Chair, Andre Dubus

Memoirs, Natalia Dolgorukaya

Memoirs, Raisa Orlova

Memoirs of a Dutiful Daughter, Simone de Beauvoir

Memoirs of Childhood and Youth, Albert Schweitzer

Memories, Dreams, Reflections, Carl G. Jung

Memories of a Catholic Girlhood, Mary McCarthy

Miriam's Kitchen: A Memoir, Elizabeth Ehrlich

Mohandas K. Gandhi: An Autobiography, the Story of My Experiments with Truth,
     Mohandas Gandhi

Motherhouse: A Novel, Jeanine Hathaway

The Names, N. Scott Momaday

Narrative of the Life of Frederick Douglass, An American Slave, Written by Himself,
     Frederick Douglass

New York Jew, Alfred Kazin

The Night Trilogy: Night, Dawn, the Accident, Elie Wiesel

Not Even My Name: A True Story, Thea Halo

Notes of a Native Son, James Baldwin

Once to Every Man: A Memoir, William Sloane Coffin

One Writer's Beginnings, Eudora Welty

Ordinary Resurrections: Children in the Years of Hope, Jonathan Kozol

Paula: A Memoir, Isabel Allende

Plant Dreaming Deep, May Sarton

The Pilgrim's Progress, John Bunyan

Poetry and Truth from My Life, Johann Wolfgang von Goethe

A Portrait of the Artist as a Young Man, James Joyce

Prescription for Survival: A Doctor's Journey to End Nuclear Madness,
     Bernard Lown, M.D.

The Promised Land—1912, Mary Antin

Reason for Hope: A Spiritual Journey, Jane Goodall

Recovering, 1978–1979, May Sarton

Refuge: An Unnatural History of Family and Place, Terry Tempest Williams

Remembrance of Things Past, Marcel Proust

Report to Greco, Nikos Kazantzakis

Returning: A Spiritual Journey, Dan Wakefield

A Romantic Education, Patricia Hampl

Salvation on Sand Mountain: Snake Handling and Redemption in Southern Appalachia,
    Dennis Covington

The Seduction of the Spirit: The Use and Misuse of People's Religion, Harvey Cox

The Seven Story Mountain, Thomas Merton

A Sort of Life, Graham Greene

Speak, Memory, Vladimir Nabokov

The Story I Tell Myself: A Venture in Existential Autobiography, Hazel E. Barnes

Surprised by Joy: The Shape of My Early Life, C. S. Lewis

Telling Secrets: A Memoir, Frederick Buechner

Things Held Dear: Soul Stories for My Sons, Roy Herron

Things Seen and Unseen: A Year Lived in Faith, Nora Gallagher

This House of Sky: Landscapes of a Western Mind, Ivan Doig

To Dwell in Peace: An Autobiography, Daniel Berrigan

Traveling Mercies: Some Thoughts on Faith, Anne Lamott

The Trembling of the Veil, William Butler Yeats

Turbulent Souls: A Catholic Son's Return to His Jewish Family, Stephen J. Dubner

An Unquiet Mind: A Memoir of Moods and Madness, Kay Redfield Jamison

Visions of Glory: A History and a Memory of Jehovah's Witnesses, Barbara G. Harrison

Walden; Cape Cod; The Maine Woods, Henry David Thoreau

A Walker in the City, Alfred Kazin

Widening Circles: A Memoir, Joanna Macy

A Woman of Egypt, Jehan Sadat

The Woman Warrior: Memoirs of a Girlhood among Ghosts, Maxine Hong Kingston

The Words: The Autobiography of Jean-Paul Sartre, Jean-Paul Sartre

Zen and the Art of Motorcycle Maintenance: An Inquiry into Values, Robert M. Pirsig

Anthologies

The Best Spiritual Writing, edited by Philip Zaleski

God: Stories, edited by C. Michael Curtis

*Searching for Your Soul: Writers of Many Faiths Share Their Personal Stories of Spiritual
    Discovery*, edited by Katherine Kurs

Till My Tale Is Told: Women's Memoirs of the Gulag, edited by S. Vilensky

Books of Particular Interest to Instructors and Workshop Leaders

Guiding Autobiography Groups for Older Adults: Exploring the Fabric of Life,
    James E. Birren and Donna E. Deutchman

The Meaning of Lives: Biography, Autobiography, and the Spiritual Quest,
    Richard A. Hutch

The Spiritual Side of Writing: Releasing the Learner's Whole Potential,
    edited by Regina Paxton Foehr and Susan A. Schiller

When Memory Speaks: Exploring the Art of Autobiography, Jill Ker Conway

Writing and Healing: Toward an Informed Practice, Charles M. Anderson
    and Marian M. MacCurdy

Writing Your Heritage: A Sequence of Thinking, Reading, and Writing Assignments,
    Debra Dixon

*Your Life as Story: Discovering the "New Autobiography" and Writing Memoir
    as Literature,* Tristine Rainer

INDEX

ABOUT THE AUTHOR

Nan Merrick Phifer deviated from past pedagogy when she taught a writing course for people who had dropped out of high school. She intuited that she could enable her students to produce meaningful writing by using as subjects their most vivid memories and greatest concerns. She encouraged hesitant writers to first pour forth their words without thought of correctness, and she followed by projecting their rough drafts onto a screen for discussion of skills and conventions. Her students' writing flourished.

Nan subsequently enrolled in the Oregon Writing Project at the University of Oregon where her strategies were confirmed. She became a codirector, and she continues to serve on the OWP Advisory Board. During her years of teaching at the secondary and college levels, Nan was made a National Teaching Fellow under Higher Education Act, Title III and granted a Certificate of Award in Recognition of Distinguished Achievement in Adult Basic Education Programs. She made presentations at many national academic conferences and wrote the textbooks *Easing into Essays, Writing Your Life: Developing Skills through Life Story Writing,* and *Writing for the Workplace.*

Now retired from college teaching, Nan presents workshops for writers' groups, libraries, religious and contemplative organizations, continuing education programs, and retreat and renewal organizations. Her lifelong interest in American literature and her Master of Liberal Arts studies at The Johns Hopkins University have contributed valuable background for her present work.

Nan's workshops range from monthly sessions in Indianapolis, where she co-guided pastors in writing to explore their vocational dedication, to a Waypoints Writing Retreat in the Rocky Mountains, to nationwide online teaching for Graduate Theological Union in Berkeley, California. At the Church of the Epiphany in Washington, DC, she guided participants in writing to design sacred space; and in a converted Coast Guard boathouse on the West Coast, she led writers in exploring the relationship between outer and inner wilderness. Currently, she is designing an innovative series of interfaith writing workshops.

To learn more about Nan's workshops and see her current calendar, please visit www.memoirworkshops.com and www.memoirworkshops.com/presentations.html.

www.Ingotpress.com